Receive Your Healing and Reclaim Your H value for those who are looking to change in health. Cal uses Scripture and his own down to business. It is time for us as Go strong and ready to live life to the fullest. Cal's book is a must for those who are ready to walk in health and live strong, the way God intended it to be.

—BENI JOHNSON
PASTOR, AUTHOR, WELLNESS SPEAKER,
AND ADVOCATE FOR HEALTHY LIVING

For many years Cal Pierce has played a lead role in promoting and demonstrating the gospel of healing and deliverance throughout this nation and around the world. His integrity and depth of understanding has been a breath of fresh air for the body of Christ. Now Cal has broached another subject that is also dear to my heart, and that is divine health. His new book, *Receive Your Healing and Reclaim Your Health*, is a phenomenal tool that will no doubt circulate around the globe to encourage, educate, and motivate Christians into a healthy lifestyle, both spiritually and naturally. In this book you will find a wealth of information concerning nutrition, exercise, and biblical insights concerning God's temple—your body. Clearly, the demands placed upon the last-days church will be considerable as we endeavor to bring in the great harvest and manifest God's kingdom in powerful and fruitful ways. We need to be healthy and strong—spirit, soul, and body. *Receive Your Healing and Reclaim Your Health* is just what we need at this crucial moment in church history, and I wholeheartedly recommend it.

—PAUL KEITH DAVIS
WHITEDOVE MINISTRIES

Cal Pierce has written one of the most timely and riveting books on health and healing. This book will literally save your life and cause you to avoid the traps many of God's people fall into regarding their health. You'll see why God not only wants you healed but also to walk in divine health so you can fully accomplish God's destiny for your life without burning out or finishing early. Loved the book!

—DAVID HERZOG
SPEAKER AND AUTHOR OF *NATURAL TO SUPERNATURAL HEALTH*
WWW.THEGLORYZONE.ORG

Cal and Michelle have addressed clear-cut vital issues concerning the stewardship of the body and the importance of being healthy in order to serve God, your family, and your fellowman to the fullest. This book is a very timely kingdom message that every individual needs to read and follow. I love the way they made this book personal, applicable, and easy to understand. Because of this teaching and the stance they have made, I believe that these two will die young at a very old age.

—Pastor Ron Williams
Author of *Faith and Fat Loss*
Natural Bodybuilder of the Decade

Cal and Michelle Pierce have powerfully impacted me through this book. Not only an impact of truth and revelation but also of actual conviction. Reading it made me want to eat healthy, live healthy, and…get delivered from gluttony (oh, yes, you must read Michelle's chapter on gluttony!). This book definitely carries key words for this hour. You will want it for your library. In fact, you might want to buy two—one to keep and one to lend.

—Patricia King
Founder of XPmedia
XPmedia.com

Receive Your Healing & Reclaim Your Health

CAL PIERCE

SILOAM

Cover design by Bill Johnson

Visit the author's website at www.healingrooms.com.

Library of Congress Cataloging-in-Publication Data
Pierce, Cal.
  Receive your healing and reclaim your health / Cal Pierce.
      p. cm.
  Includes bibliographical references (p.   ).
  ISBN 978-1-61638-483-8 (trade paper) -- ISBN 978-1-61638-703-7
(e-book) 1. Health--Religious aspects--Christianity. I. Title.
  BT732.P54 2012
  261.8'321--dc23

                          2011040317

12 13 14 15 16 — 9 8 7 6 5 4 3 2 1
Printed in the United States of America

Contents

Chapter 1

THE CONDITION OF THE BODY

*The condition we are in is determined
by the position we take.*

As I begin to write this book, I cannot help but think about the unhealthy condition of the body of Christ. I see so many who are unhealthy and sick. As director of Healing Rooms Ministries, I travel the world to minister healing to the body of Christ. In spite of my efforts and those of many others to minister healing, it seems that I see as many unhealthy and sick people today as I saw when I began in this ministry eleven years ago. This sad reality is a huge concern to me. The wonderful healing results we see in the lives of people to whom we minister does not seem to make a dent in the growing need for healing. And for some who receive healing, their lifestyles continue to be so unhealthy that they become sick again.

A Need to Refocus

Many sincere and successful ministers of what we call the "healing movement" have focused almost entirely on eradicating sickness through prayer. They have not considered our responsibility for healthy living, the stewardship of our bodies. They have reasoned that we only deal with spiritual realities of divine healing. The truth is that we need to refocus on the truths of physical stewardship for the body. Unfortunately, for many, these truths do not seem "spiritual"; they believe that only supernatural, divine healing is spiritual.

We have not understood clearly that God's ultimate goal is not the healing of symptoms of sickness. His goal is the ultimate provision for healing that results in a healthy spirit, soul, and body—with no sickness. We do not get healed from a physical ailment to get sick again, do we? Yet if we focus only on healing, we just deal with the *symptoms* of an unhealthy body. We need to refocus our thinking so that we can get healed and stay that way.

Perhaps you are wondering, "Aren't there diseases we can get even if we are healthy?" The simple answer is no. A healthy person has an immune system that, when strong, protects it from all manner of disease. When we are healthy, as born-again believers, we not only have a *physical* immunity but a *spiritual* immunity as well. The scriptures teach that Christ redeemed us from the curse of the Law, so that the blessing of Abraham might come to us:

> Christ redeemed us from the curse of the Law, having become a curse for us…in order that in Christ Jesus the blessing of Abraham might come to the Gentiles, so that we would receive the promise of the Spirit through faith.
>
> —GALATIANS 3:13–14

The curse from which Christ redeemed us entered through the sin of Adam and Eve when they disobeyed God's command in the Garden of Eden. Then, when the Law of Moses was given, which man could not keep, Scripture says, "Cursed is everyone who does not abide by all things written in the book of the Law, to perform them" (Gal. 3:10). Sickness, as well as separation from God, was a part of that curse. The prophet Isaiah understood that God was redeeming us from sin and sickness through Christ's death when he prophesied: "He was crushed for our iniquities…and by His scourging we are healed" (Isa. 53:5). The apostle Peter reiterated this wonderful promise for healing:

…and He Himself bore our sins in His body on the cross, so that we might die to sin and live to righteousness; for by His wounds you were healed.

—1 PETER 2:24

If we have been redeemed from sickness, then why are we bearing the sickness Jesus already bore for us? Didn't Jesus bear the sickness so we would not have to? Jesus said, "You will know the truth, and the truth will make you free" (John 8:32). One of the problems is that we cannot accept truth if we do not know it. We cannot wrap our mind around a truth to which our mind has not been *renewed*.

The Need for Renewal

If we are to walk in continual health, our minds need to be renewed to God's will for our health. The apostle Paul taught us how to know the will of God:

And do not be conformed to this world, but be transformed by the renewing of your mind, that you may prove what the will of God is, that which is good and acceptable and perfect.

—ROMANS 12:2

Unfortunately, we *have* been conformed to the world's order of what health should look like, as well as how to obtain it. We are offered all kinds of diets, exercise devices, and wellness programs that promise to provide us with optimal health. Yet studies show that nearly 70 percent of the population of the United States is overweight.[1] In spite of enjoying one of the most advanced medical systems in the world, we are some of the unhealthiest people on earth.

"Unhealth" Statistics

- The US Centers for Disease Control and Prevention (CDC) estimate that 26.7 percent of our population is obese.[2]

- This means that approximately 73 million adults are obese, making them at risk for coronary heart disease, hypertension, stroke, type 2 diabetes, certain types of cancer, and premature death.[3]

- The CDC also estimates the medical care costs of obesity in the United States to total $147 billion.[4]

We live in a society where profit motives drive our food industry. Our grocery stores are filled with processed foods that are void of nutrition. Artificial flavors and additives such as high-fructose corn syrup and other processed sugars are added for taste. These sweeteners alone are one of the greatest sources of calories in our diet today.

Sugar: Sweet or Dangerous?

According to the US Department of Agriculture (USDA), Americans consume 156 pounds of added sugar per person each year; that is thirty-one 5-pound bags for each of us.[5] Only about 29 pounds of it comes as traditional sugar, according to the Sugar Association; the rest comes from "foods"—or what we call foods: candy, soda, and junk food, as well as unlikely sources like crackers, yogurt, ketchup, and peanut butter.[6]

For perspective, at the turn of the twentieth century (1900), sugar consumption amounted to only five pounds per person.[7] It is also interesting to consider that in the early 1900s cardiovascular disease and cancer were not nearly as prevalent as they are today.

I have come to believe that sugar is one of the most dangerous, addictive substances we can consume. One inherent danger in consuming large amounts of refined sugar is that it raises the insulin level, which inhibits the release of growth hormones and in turn depresses the immune system. A depressed immune system cannot protect the body from sickness and disease; it is that simple.

God created our bodies to metabolize the food we eat to create energy. Food is the fuel that drives our bodies. Refined dietary sugars lack minerals and vitamins. Instead of fueling our bodies properly, they are metabolized into fat cells around such vital organs as the heart, stomach, and liver. Consuming such faulty "fuels" makes us unhealthy. Then we discover that we need medical treatment.

The World's Method to Regain Health

Unfortunately, as a nation we have developed a medical approach that is a *disease management system* rather than a true *health care system*. We go to the doctor who diagnoses the health problem we have, often caused by our unhealthy lifestyle. Drug companies sell drugs (complete with side effects) to "manage" our health problems. The doctor prescribes the appropriate drugs for our symptoms; we keep eating unhealthy foods and gaining weight, and the "cycle of unhealth" continues.

As we get older and continue to live in this unhealthy cycle, we become more and more malnourished with a weakened immune system. We do not have energy to exercise; without exercise we gain more weight, which results in more serious disease. Through a lack of exercise and continued weight gain, our joints are forced to "carry the burden." Without proper muscle support, our joints fail, and we schedule joint replacement surgery. Does this sound like the normal American life, aging with predictable health issues and conforming to the world's method of treatment for them?

In contrast, the Bible teaches us how to be healed and walk in health. We need to search out this truth of what divine healing produces: a body that has no sickness, is healed, and walks in health. To regain our health, we need to renew our minds with the truth of the Word. A renewed mind does not think the way it used to think; it believes the truth. We are set free to live a lifestyle of health as we choose to become stewards of our bodies and walk in obedience to the truth.

Choose Life

What is amazing to me is that none of this unhealthy American lifestyle is necessary. Our *life* does not determine our *lifestyle*; our *lifestyle* determines our *life*. By *life*, I am referring to the quality of health you enjoy in body, mind, and spirit. Too many people have a bad life because their lifestyles engage them in wrong thoughts, attitudes, and actions. For example, when my lifestyle was devoid of good nutritional and exercise habits, my entire life became unhealthy.

In my journey to regain my health, I have come to realize that it takes a lot more effort to be *sick* than to be *healthy*. To be sick, you just do what feels good, which seems effortless, right? But your "effortless" choices never satisfy and require more and more from you, ending in pain, sickness, doctor visits, drugs, and medical expenses you cannot afford. Now that's effort!

To be healthy, in the beginning you have to choose to eat right and to exercise properly. Seems like real effort. But whether you choose to be sick or to be healthy, it is going to cost you something. One choice leads to abundant life; the other leads to ongoing misery.

The purpose of this book is to encourage you to choose to become healthy by allowing your mind to be renewed with God's health care system. You can learn that your chronological age does not determine your health; it is your choices that determine your health. If you are healthy, you will not need medical treatment.

Jesus said, "It is not those who are healthy who need a physician, but those who are sick" (Matt. 9:12). In context, He was explaining that He came to save those who are sin-sick, not those who did not see their need for a physician. Still, the fact remains that when you are healthy, you have no need of a doctor.

Keep in mind that when Jesus said, "The Son of Man has come to save that which was lost" (Matt. 18:11), the Greek word He used for *saved* means "to be completely whole."[8] The lady with the issue of blood decided to touch the hem of Jesus's garment because she said to herself that if she could do so, she would "get well" (Matt. 9:21). The phrase "get well" is translated from that same word *sozo*. She knew by faith that she would be completely whole if she could just touch Jesus. Jesus died to redeem not just our spirit, but also the temple of His body that we are, which houses the Holy Spirit.

Our goal should be to become healthy so that we will not need a physician. I am not saying physicians are bad. Quite the contrary, their goal is to get you well. I have never met a physician who was not happy to see their patient restored to good health. My doctor is always happy to see me in good health when he gives me my physical. As a matter of fact, he always asks me what I am doing to stay so healthy at sixty-six years of age. The key to life is to get to a place where we do not need medical treatment because of poor lifestyle choices that are undermining our health. Our doctor cannot make those choices for us.

I chose life.

At sixty-two years of age I had to acknowledge that I was in a very unhealthy condition. I was the director of an international healing ministry, rejoicing in the ministry God had given me. Yet I had gained so much weight that I was considered obese according to the body mass index (BMI). Largely as a result of my obesity, I suffered a heart attack.

This health crisis was a real wake-up call for me. Before the heart attack, I realized that I had become very weak because of my unhealthy lifestyle. I remember that I had to grip a chair hard and push myself up with my arms to get out of a chair. My legs were so weak that I could not stand up without assisting them with my arms. I wondered, "How did I get to this point?" I was in bad shape, and after the heart attack, I finally recognized it.

In my desperation, I asked the Holy Spirit to reveal to me what the problem was and how to fix it. He wasted no time in responding to my question. I heard the Holy Spirit first say, "Your problem began when you thought you had a life. This 'house,' your physical body, doesn't belong to you; it is God's house." He reminded me of the apostle Paul's assertion:

> I have been crucified with Christ; and it is no longer I who live, but Christ lives in me; and the life which I now live in the flesh I live by faith in the Son of God, who loved me and gave Himself up for me.
>
> —GALATIANS 2:20

Then He took me to Romans 8:6 and reminded me that "the mind set on the flesh is death, but the mind set on the Spirit is life and peace." Wow! In that moment I realized that I really thought I had a life. I had not considered, in the area of my health, the biblical reality that "...your body is a temple of the Holy Spirit who is in you, whom you have from God, and that you are not your own? For you have been bought with a price: therefore glorify God in your body" (1 Cor. 6:19–20).

When it came to eating and exercise, I forgot about the Spirit of God, who wants to live in me. I found it easy to set my mind on my flesh; it always wanted my attention. It was easy to eat that tub of popcorn with a cube of butter on it. I loved those scones I ate daily with my coffee at Starbucks. Those "delicacies" made my flesh feel good. I did not realize how much my mind was "set on my flesh" or the death that was threatening me as a result.

Now, I began to realize that there was constant communication between the two. My flesh "told" my mind, "You don't need to exercise; it doesn't feel good. You never did it in the past, so why do it now?" My flesh always wanted what was easy. In my health crisis, I finally discovered that what is *easy* may not be the best for me. *Dying* is easy; it does not require any effort to curb your flesh or your mind. It is living that is hard; you have to work at it. First, you have to determine to allow the Word of God to renew your mind to think God's thoughts and let His truth set you free.

What I am saying is that for years during my life's journey, I had set my mind on the flesh, feeding it what it desired. That unhealthy lifestyle resulted in a heart attack that brought me to the door of death. And the Holy Spirit reminded me, "The mind set on the flesh is death" (Rom. 8:6). Lying there, at the door of death, I was ready to listen. The Holy Spirit showed me clearly that I had to reset my mind. It had to be renewed so that I would set my mind on the Spirit, which brings life and peace (v. 6).

I was in trouble, and I knew it. I knew something had to change, or I could die. At this point I knew dying would be much easier than living; my mind had to be renewed so that I could change what I was doing that had brought me to the point of death. Relentlessly, in His love, the Holy Spirit said to me, "I can't renew your mind until you reset it. I can't renew a mind that is set on the flesh. That mind will fulfill the desires of the flesh and work against Me."

> But I say, walk by the Spirit, and you will not carry out the desire of the flesh. For the flesh sets its desire against the Spirit, and the

> Spirit against the flesh; for these are in opposition to one another, so that you may not do the things that you please.
>
> —GALATIANS 5:16–17

As a minister, I knew the Word of God was true; I had believed its power for the healing of many people. Yet I thought it was impossible for me to become healthy and strong in a culture that continually tempted me with foods that were not good for me. It seemed normal to adopt the lifestyle cycle of eating unhealthy foods, getting fat, going on a diet, trying an exercise program, failing in those attempts, and giving up in discouragement. I simply believed that diets did not work.

It seemed to me that every week there was a new exercise device advertised on TV. I concluded, "That must be an indication they don't work either." From that defeated mind-set I would have to reset my mind from what does not work in the world to what does work in the kingdom of God. How was I to do that? The Holy Spirit was not done answering my questions. He directed me to this wonderful truth:

> Therefore if you have been raised up with Christ, keep seeking the things above, where Christ is, seated at the right hand of God. Set your mind on the things above, not on the things that are on earth.
>
> —COLOSSIANS 3:1–2

I was setting my mind on the things that did not work, concluding that changing my unhealthy lifestyle was impossible. But God says to keep seeking the things above where Christ is. I knew that the Word teaches if I seek the Holy Spirit, then all things will become possible (Matt. 19:26). Until that point, what I was doing in serving my flesh seemed right to me. Even if it wasn't, I thought I had no other options. The Holy Spirit reminded me that it is natural to think we are right:

> There is a way which seems right to man, but its end is the way
> of death.
>
> —Proverbs 16:25

I began to understand that my mind was set in a wrong place. When I fed my flesh, it felt good. I thought it was OK, but it was killing me, slowly but surely, one day at a time. Isn't it interesting that we do not mind dying slowly? We just do not want to die suddenly. That is where I found myself, slowly destroying my life with an unhealthy lifestyle. I did not get worried until I realized that I could die suddenly. I was focused on healing from my damaged heart, not on what healing produces—a body that is truly healed.

Understanding the Terms

In my sphere of relationships, in churches or outside of them, it seemed that no one wanted to address the real health issues regarding our responsibility to be stewards of "the temple of God." We only wanted to talk about healing of the symptoms caused by our unhealthy lifestyles. As the Holy Spirit continued to teach me, I began to see that ministering divine healing or receiving healing as promised in the Scriptures has always pointed to this larger issue of *walking in health*.

The dictionary defines the word *heal* as: "make sound or whole, to restore to health, to return to a sound state."[9] *Health* is defined as "being sound in body, mind, and spirit; freedom from physical disease."[10] *Healing* is the *process* of relieving the body of sickness so that the body is restored to wholeness; i.e., no sickness.[11] Health is living life from a position of freedom from disease.

In the Bible, the main Hebrew word translated "healing" means "health, cure, sound."[12] It is used in the wonderful promise of God: "But for you who fear My name, the sun of righteousness will rise with healing in its wings" (Mal. 4:2). Again, there is a direct connection between physical healing and a reverential fear of God that causes us to walk in His ways.

In the New Testament, the main word translated from the Greek as "healing" is *therapeia*, which means "to heal, cure, restore to health."[13] You can probably recognize our English word *therapy* there, which is "therapeutic treatment especially of bodily...disorder."[14]

When you have been sick and are healed, your body is restored to health; i.e., cured, no sickness remains. In short, we can conclude that your need for *healing* refers to your physical *condition* and remedies it; *health* refers to your *position* in life after you are healed. You may wonder why I am emphasizing the difference between the terms *healing* and *health*. It is because your need for *healing* is often a result of your lack of understanding of the larger issues of *health* as I explained in sharing about my unhealthy lifestyle that led to my life-and-death health crisis. It is the will of God, as revealed in both the Old and New Testaments, for you to walk in health:

> "For I will restore you to health, and I will heal you of your wounds," declares the LORD.
>
> —JEREMIAH 30:17

> Beloved, I pray that in all respects you may prosper and be in good health, just as your soul prospers.
>
> —3 JOHN 2

In order for your soul to prosper, as I mentioned, your mind will have to be renewed to the truth that your body is a temple of God and you are responsible to care for it and respect it as such. You need to accept the biblical reality that you are not your own; you do not have a life to throw away by indulging the desires of your flesh.

Notice in Jeremiah 30:17 God says He "will restore you to health." How will God restore us to health? He will heal us of our wounds.

But, especially if our wounds are a result of self-inflicted lifestyle choices, He does not just heal us so we can do what we want and get sick again. God's stated goal was, "You shall be My people, and I will be your God" (v. 22). In essence, God said in that passage that His goal for His people is "to restore you to health so that your focus is on Me and on what you need to do to please Me and honor Me with your body, mind, and spirit."

A new day

It was a new day for me when I began to believe that I could walk in divine health. I believe the body of Christ is coming to a place where the Word that we read will become the Word that we *live*. We will begin to choose life and to have faith that we can live without sickness. I think the problem is that we have not believed we could walk in health, without sickness. I know I did not believe that I could walk in health before my heart attack.

As I sought God for understanding, the Holy Spirit continued to ask me some very interesting questions that I could not answer. He first asked me: "Do you believe that Jesus redeemed you from all of the curse or only some of it?" As I pondered the question, He showed me 1 John 1:9: "If we confess our sins, He is faithful and righteous to forgive us our sins and to cleanse us from all unrighteousness." I understood that "*all* unrighteousness" included my wrong thinking about my health condition.

He said to me, "You have been redeemed from all of the curse, including sickness. What Adam lost, Jesus redeemed." Then He asked me, "Why would you bear the sickness Jesus bore for you?" I understood that Jesus was my substitute; He bore all my sin and my sickness so that I would not have to. I realized that in my mind my *position* was wrong. I thought it was all right to bear my "sickness" of obesity; it seemed even normal according to the culture in which I lived. I had determined my *position* based on my unhealthy *condition*.

I began to understand that, regarding my unhealthy lifestyle, my *position* had to be based on the Word of God, not my circumstances or cultural tastes. I knew the Word said, "You shall know the truth, and the truth shall make you free" (John 8:32, NKJV). Well, I was not free. After my heart attack, I knew my health was going downhill fast. It never occurred to me that God's truth would bring me to a position where I could live in a truly healthy condition.

Not All Sickness Is a Result of Unhealthy Lifestyles

The work of the cross to redeem us from the curse of sickness is available to every person who accepts Christ as Savior. Whether your physical malady is a result of lifestyle choices, accidents, or genetic diseases, God's desire is that every person receive their healing. He loves all His children and offers His miracles of healing and health to them, no matter how they got sick.

I don't mean for this message on *positioning* yourself for living in health to be intimidating to someone who is sick. I want to help you realize God's will for His children is health. He loves you so much that He sent His Son Jesus to redeem you from the curse of sickness. He provided your healing supernaturally, through His death and resurrection, so that you can experience the blessing of health.

As I mentioned, the prophet Isaiah declared this truth, though the translators for the King James Version did not properly connect *physical* healing with Christ's bearing our *griefs* and *sorrows*. The original Hebrew word for *griefs* means "sickness"[15] and the word for *sorrows* means "pain, physical or mental."[16] Isaiah's prophetic declaration is more accurately translated as follows:

> Surely He has borne our griefs (*sicknesses, weaknesses, and distresses*) and carried our *sorrows and pains*.... He was wounded for our transgressions, He was bruised for our guilt and iniquities;

the chastisement [needful to obtain] peace and well-being for us was upon Him, and with the stripes [that wounded] Him we are healed and made whole.

—ISAIAH 53:4–5, AMP, EMPHASIS ADDED

Sickness is the devil's business.

Jesus is our Healer; He is not our afflicter. The devil is our afflicter, the author of sickness; God is the author of healing and health. God never created us to be sick. In Genesis, God never said, "Let there be sickness." As I studied the Scriptures, I began to see how sickness originated. It came as a result of sin that entered through mankind's disobedience to God's command. Jesus came to redeem us from *all* the results of that sin of Adam and Eve in the garden. He taught us, "The thief comes only to steal and kill and destroy; I came that they may have life, and have it abundantly" (John 10:10).

We see the fulfillment of Isaiah's prophecy in the life of Jesus:

When evening came, they brought to Him many who were demon-possessed; and He cast out the spirits with a word, and healed all who were ill. This was to fulfill what was spoken through Isaiah the prophet: "He Himself took our infirmities and carried away our diseases."

—MATTHEW 8:16–17

God's will is that Isaiah's prophecy be fulfilled in our lives today. That is, Jesus already took our infirmities and carried away our diseases through His death on the cross. I always had difficulty with this truth because I did not see it lived out in the body of Christ. I thought, "This can't be true because I see so many sick people in the church." The problem with this faulty thinking is that it is based in a belief system that lines up with the will of the enemy, not the will of God.

Unfortunately, I was believing that the devil had the power to make me sick, but I could not believe that God, who has greater power, could make me well. My mind was accepting the will of the enemy rather than the truth of God that could set me free. Then the Holy Spirit said to me, "You will justify the beliefs on which you set your mind." I began to recognize my problem of believing the lie of the enemy rather than Christ's finished work on Calvary.

I received a letter from a pastor that really spoke to the problem we see in the body of Christ regarding our responsibility of stewardship of our bodies to walk in health. He wrote:

> Dear Brother Pierce,
>
> I have been on a journey of late to address how much time we spend asking for the healing of the saints who are struggling with diabetes, obesity, high blood pressure, etc., when in fact we have brought much of this sickness upon ourselves. I was very excited by your article "The Kingdom Health Care System: The Marriage of Health and Healing in the Body of Christ." I have been led to put together more teaching for our local body of Christ in this area of need.
>
> A little about myself. I have been a pastor for thirty-seven years and have in recent years suffered a six-way heart bypass, type 2 diabetes, obesity, etc. I have been making changes that will be practical helps for my health...I have lost 50 pounds so far, taken up cycling (I can ride sixty to seventy miles at a time), and I am a vegetarian now. I am not trying to turn my church into vegans or vegetarians, but I am weary of seeing my brothers and sisters slowly have years stolen from their lives by their poor life choices. I know how easily this can come across as legalistic, but I am tired of seeing years stolen from normally productive saints. I would be interested in any seminar or books you could recommend to me. I have a large library of health books (not diet books) and hope to find a true spiritual understanding of God's plan for His body and how to care for the physical temple, while we are pursuing the spiritual walk with our Lord and Savior.

This pastor's letter testifies to choices we can make to steward our bodies into health. With God, it is never too late. All things are possible with God. No matter how out of shape we are, when we partner with God, His healing power will restore us to health. When we obey His Word, it is medicine that can restore us to health:

> My son, give attention to my words; incline your ear to my sayings. Do not let them depart from your sight; keep them in the midst of your heart. For they are *life* to those who find them and health to *all* their body.
> —PROVERBS 4:20–23, EMPHASIS ADDED

In this scripture the word *life* means "living, revival, sustenance, renewal."[17] This divine recovery is to *all* our body. Therefore, if we apply the Word of God to our pursuit of health, it will sustain us to reach our goal. The Word becomes the medicine for our healing and health. The New Testament teaches clearly the health benefits of living a disciplined life, obeying the Word of God:

> Therefore, strengthen the hands that are weak and the knees that are feeble, and make straight paths for your feet, so that the limb which is lame may not be put out of joint, but rather be healed.
> —HEBREWS 12:12–13

The Word of God here is encouraging us to strengthen ourselves so that we can run the race with endurance. Hebrews 12:10 tells us that our earthly fathers disciplined us according to what seemed best to them, but that God disciplines us for our good, that we may share His holiness. Discipline establishes strength and endurance in our lives. As we give attention to the Word of God, He gives us the life that we need to receive our healing and begin to walk in health.

When Jesus demonstrated the kingdom of God on the earth through healing, it was an indication He wanted a church, His body on the earth, that had no sickness in it. Considering what we have been redeemed from, should the body of Christ be sick? If Jesus bore our sin and sickness, why should we? The apostle Paul taught:

> But if the Spirit of Him who raised Jesus from the dead dwells in you, He who raised Christ Jesus from the dead will also give life to your mortal bodies through His Spirit who dwells in you.
> —ROMANS 8:11

When Paul declares the power of putting on the armor of God, He said that God gives us the shield of faith, "with which you will be able to extinguish all the flaming arrows of the evil one" (Eph. 6:16). Is sickness one of those flaming arrows? Does God tell us that with His armor we can extinguish *all* of those arrows? Emphatically, yes! God is telling us that His armor will provide the power to overcome sickness so that we can begin to walk in health. Walking in divine health is simply walking without sin or sickness; it is the fullness of redemption.

Unfortunately, this life of wholeness is not currently manifest in the church! The questions we need to ask ourselves are: "Can we become healthy? Is this God's will for us? With the power of God and a renewed mind, can we achieve good health?" This issue of renewing our minds to believe the Word of God is vital to achieving the promises of God for our health:

> For as he thinks within himself, so he is.
> —PROVERBS 23:7

According to the Scriptures, we will become what we think. The apostle Paul exhorted all believers to "present your bodies a living and holy sacrifice, acceptable to God, which is your spiritual service of worship. And do not be conformed to this world, but be *transformed by the renewing of your mind*, so that you may prove what the will of God is, that which is good and acceptable and perfect" (Rom. 12:1–2, emphasis added). The way we can prove the will of God for our health is to think within ourselves that we can become healthy. Our transformed thinking will empower us to obtain the goal.

Only with a renewed mind can we think differently. As our mind is renewed to the will of God, we begin to think according to His will for us. That is when we receive the promise of Jesus that *all* things are possible to him who believes (Mark 9:23). In the next chapter I want to share with you some of my painful journey from sickness to health as I allowed God to transform my thinking.

Chapter 2

MY JOURNEY

Failure requires a decision backed up by no effort.

We began our Healing Rooms Ministries when I was fifty-five years old. At the time of this writing, I am sixty-six years old. I have always been active in life and in ministry. I have never been one to sit still for very long. Even when Michelle and I would take a vacation, we would sit on the beach for only a short time before looking at our watches and saying to each other, "What can we do next?"

During these past eleven years of ministry, we have established more than thirteen hundred healing rooms in fifty-three nations. In addition, I have traveled extensively, hosting at least twenty conferences annually to cast the vision for the establishing of healing rooms. When I am at home, I spend most of my time in our headquarters' offices. I love being with our staff and ministry team with whom we have become a "kingdom family." Mine is not a sedentary, solitary lifestyle.

Becoming Weak

Most of my life I have considered myself to be in good health. I never liked to go to doctors or to take medicine. I always expected that I would be in good health. Then I began to notice unexpected weight gain. My mobility was affected, and I had to push to get up from a chair. I noticed my legs grew tired and I was out of breath when climbing stairs. In short, I was experiencing weakness for the first time in my life.

I had never focused on my personal health, perhaps because I was in a healing ministry. I guess I thought if I had a problem, God would heal me. It never occurred to me that it might be wrong thinking to put anything I wanted into my body and expect God to take care of it. Suddenly here I was, feeling weak and unhealthy.

Falling to temptation

In the garden of Gethsemane, when Jesus's disciples fell asleep, He cautioned them, "Keep watching and praying that you may not come into temptation; the spirit is willing, but the flesh is weak" (Mark 14:38). I began to realize that I had "come into temptation" regarding food because I was not praying about health or watching what I was eating. I fed my body what it wanted. My spirit "was willing"; I wanted to have a healthy body.

Unfortunately, I was experiencing the truth of Jesus's words: "the flesh is weak." I did not realize that the power to overcome the flesh in any area, including health, is achieved by setting my mind on the Spirit and watching and praying. I had only applied this biblical truth to my spiritual growth, not my "health growth."

I then began to talk to the Holy Spirit about my physical health. His first response was, "You have only have one body; if you mess it up, you are out." Then He said, "If you mess it up, we are both out." I thought of the scripture that tells us we are the temple of the Holy Spirit:

> Do you not know that you are a temple of God, and that the Spirit of God dwells in you? If any man destroys the temple of God, God will destroy him, for the temple of God is holy, and that is what you are.
>
> —1 Corinthians 3:16–17

I began to realize that the Holy Spirit did not come to dwell in my body because He was homeless and needed a place to stay. He is in me for the fulfillment of the will of God through my life. That makes it very important that I stick around. Because the Holy Spirit lives in me—I am the temple in which He dwells—He has as much interest in my being healthy as I do. He pointed out the fact that if I could become a *spiritual* giant, what good is that if I become physically unhealthy, get sick, and die. I began to understand that a triune God—Father, Son, and Holy Spirit—wants to impact a triune man—spirit, mind, and body.

My lifestyle regarding food was threatening my life, which would negatively impact my destiny in God. I had yielded to temptation in giving in to the desires of my flesh in unhealthy eating habits. The apostle Paul's words suddenly took on new meaning:

> For those who are according to the flesh set their minds on the things of the flesh, but those who are according to the Spirit, the things of the Spirit. For the mind set on the flesh is death, but the mind set on the Spirit is life and peace.
>
> —ROMANS 8:5–6

Paul declared bluntly that "the mind set on the flesh is death." The Greek word translated "death" carries the connotation of "poisonous or will cause to be that way."[1] Sickness can be described as incipient death or death in progress. I was weak, physically, because I allowed my mind to indulge the desires of the flesh. One of those desires resulted in my overindulgence of food, which was making me fat and weak. At the time I did not realize that I had applied this scripture to my spiritual life only. If I had a health problem, I attributed that to my natural life, to which I felt the Bible did not apply.

That kind of faulty thinking almost killed me. I did not realize that I had a responsibility to the Spirit of God, who dwells in me, to steward His temple. The Holy Spirit asked me a question: "Whose body are you?" The Spirit dwelling within us gives us the power to overcome the flesh and to cause the flesh to line up with the will of God. Understanding this truth was the key that allowed me to overcome my weakness. I began to understand that I could partner with the Holy Spirit to become strong—both spiritually and physically.

My wrong attitude about food

When my mind was set on the flesh, I would focus on eating anything that felt good. I loved sweets, fried food, any kind of bread, and, of course, popcorn with lots of butter. As a matter of fact, popcorn was one of my favorite foods as a child. I remember my mom putting me on a stool so that I could reach to shake the pan of popcorn seed on the stove to keep it from burning.

I had my favorite popcorn pan that I always used. When I got married, my mother wrapped that pan and gave it to me as one of my wedding gifts. I would eat a full pan of popcorn with an entire cube of butter on it. After Michelle and I got married, we would go to the theater just to buy the buttered popcorn and take it home to eat, without watching a movie.

It seemed that every time I turned around, there was a food that I loved staring at me. When we began Healing Rooms Ministries, which required a large staff, that temptation only increased. With a staff and team of more than one hundred fifty people, we were celebrating a birthday or anniversary two or three times a week. Of course, we have to celebrate with cake and cookies. Then there are the potluck dinners at the office where there are more fat-producing foods than any one person should eat.

Without exercising any discipline in the area of eating, I began to put on the pounds. I did not pay attention to my ominous weight gain until I noticed I could not button my pants. Then I thought I would simply go on a diet to solve the problem. Upon investigation, I found there were so many diets I did not have a clue where to start. And I noticed that everyone I talked to about dieting was an "expert" on the subject.

So I would try a diet that someone suggested. A few days after beginning the diet, we would have a staff potluck dinner. I would go through the food line with my plate, passing up all the "good" (bad) food and filling my plate with the salads. Just as I was beginning to feel good about my victory, I arrived at the dessert section. In the middle of the dessert table is one piece of chocolate pudding pie, my favorite. There is only one piece, and it is sitting there looking at me.

I am standing there looking back, and in my mind I begin to have a conversation with this piece of pie. I am convinced there are demons in sweets, "controlling spirits" that talk to you. The pie says:

> Look at me. I am your favorite. You love me, don't you? You even told your staff I am your favorite. You told your wife that you love me. And you realize I am the last piece. You might as well eat me. After all, I know you are starting your diet, and one last piece of pie won't hurt.

I was standing there thinking (my first mistake), "I can't believe I am having a conversation with a piece of chocolate pudding pie." And the conversation was not over. The pie then says:

> Look, I have that flaky piecrust you like so much. Remember, when you were driving to the potluck and your wife told you Maribeth had made you your favorite pie? Well, here I am. As a matter of fact, Maribeth is probably looking at you right now to see if you take me; if you don't, she will be hurt. Look, there is a table with no one sitting at it. You can take me over there, eat your pie, then move to the tables with your friends with just your salads and look good.

That argument was so convincing that I knew of only one way to get rid of that "sweet demon"—*I ate it!* That is pretty much the scenario of my failure cycle in yielding to temptation every time I started a diet. Food had control over my life; I had a love relationship with food. I would tell Michelle I love this food or that food.

The Holy Spirit warned me, "You can't be delivered from what you love." Then He said, "If you will love Me, you won't have to love food." I began to understand that food had become my "comforter" rather than the Holy Spirit, who is called the Comforter in the Scriptures. Jesus said:

> If you [really] love Me, you will keep (obey) My commands. And I will ask the Father, and He will give you another Comforter (Counselor, Helper, Intercessor, Advocate, Strengthener and Standby), that He may remain with you forever—the Spirit of Truth...
>
> —John 14:15–17, amp

A Wake-Up Call—Heart Attack

My love relationship with food eventually led to a health crisis. The problem presented itself when I was speaking at a national Healing Rooms Conference in Holland. We had just finished a morning meeting and were on our way upstairs to a room where our hosts had prepared lunch. As my wife, Michelle, and I were going up the stairs with members of our team, I began to lose my breath; my chest felt tight. By the time I had climbed to the top of the stairs, I could hardly walk to the lunchroom.

Seeing my distress, our national director guided me to a couch to rest and see if these frightening symptoms were only temporary. Instead, they got worse, and everyone began to pray. One of our directors in Holland is a doctor. Friends summoned him to examine me. His immediate diagnosis was that I was having a heart attack and needed to go the hospital immediately.

I said, "Well, let's get in a car and go." The doctor informed me that in Holland, when someone is having symptoms, the law requires an ambulance for transportation." I was thinking, "This is not my idea of what should happen when I am the speaker at a national healing conference. Can't I quietly go out the back door, get into a car, go to the hospital, get the problem fixed, and return for the evening meeting?" Of course, everyone was praying, "God, we need divine intervention."

In a few moments I heard the distinctive on-and-off sound of a European ambulance approaching. Soon, in walked the paramedics carrying a gurney. And I was thinking, "Oh, God, blind the eyes of all those people downstairs when I am wheeled past them. What on earth are they going to think when the healing evangelist is wheeled to an ambulance?" I was thankful that we found a side door through which to exit to the ambulance. The paramedics placed me inside and began the drive to the hospital, with Michelle joining me while some of our team members followed.

You cannot imagine the confused thoughts I was having: "God, is this a test or something? If it is, can't it wait until I am home? I don't know what kind of professional care they give in Holland." Meanwhile Michelle is praying and talking to me on the way to the hospital. I am telling her, "I don't need this. I have things to do." It never occurred to me that I could die. I only hoped the hospital had someone qualified enough to fix the problem.

When we arrived at the hospital, the paramedics opened the back doors and begin pulling the gurney out. The next thing that was supposed to happen was for the gurney wheels to drop into place. Well, that did not happen. Instead *I* dropped to the ground. I hit so hard that if I had not been hanging onto the side rails, I would have bounced off the gurney onto the ground. My next thought was, "Oh, God, deliver me!" The medics lifted the gurney, fiddled with the mechanism awhile to get the wheels in place, and then wheeled me away quickly.

I was crashing through double doors, heading to the emergency room, just like you may have seen on TV. Michelle and the team were running after me asking me how I was doing. Then Michelle was diverted to a desk to sign me into the hospital while I went into a room for a medical test. At this point I was watching everyone very carefully and praying, "God, do they know what they are doing?"

When the test was finished, medical personnel told me I had suffered a heart attack and needed to have a stent placed into an artery. I told the nurse, "That's fine; I will be home next week and can have it put in then." She gave me that look a mother gives to a ten-year-old who has said something wrong. She answered, "You need the stent now. They are getting an operating room ready for the surgery."

Her surprising announcement gave me a whole new meaning of what it means to put your life into God's hands. The next thing I knew, I was being wheeled into surgery. I meet a young doctor who had one nurse with him. I was thinking, "Where is the team of doctors and nurses? You mean there are just two of you?" He asked me if I wanted to be put asleep or to stay awake for the procedure. I asked, "Will it hurt?" He said, "Not really. We will simply go through a small incision in the groin through an artery to where the block is and install the stent." He said he would give me an injection to deaden nerves at the entry point. And if I opted to stay awake, I could watch the whole procedure on the monitor.

I opted to stay awake. I wanted to keep an eye on this guy. Actually, the whole procedure went very well. I watched the stent move through the artery until it reached the blockage. As it moved into the blockage, I could feel the pressure relieved. He then said, "That's all there is to it; we are finished." It had all seemed so simple. I thanked God as I was wheeled to my hospital room.

Mistaken Identity?

Now I was ready to go home. I asked the nurse when I could check out so that we could arrange a flight back home. She replied, "You must stay in the hospital for three days, and you cannot fly for seven days after this procedure." I do not know which was more stressful, having the stent put into my artery or having to sit around for a week before flying home. Of course, I could count on my wife, Michelle, to deliver her famous quote to me: "You'll live!"

So here I was stuck in this hospital for three days. I noticed the other patients were wearing pajamas. I found out that in Holland, they do no supply them; you bring your sleepwear from home. Well, needless to say, I had not had time to do that. So when I awoke in the morning, I put my street clothes on and lay on top of the bed. Throughout the day people were coming into my room, shaking my hand and greeting me. I thought, "The people in Holland are sure friendly."

When I got up to walk down the hall, people would stop and say "hi" in Dutch, shake my hand, and then go about their business. Not until I was checking out of the hospital did I discover the reason for their friendliness. The lady in the business office spoke good English, so I commented about how friendly everyone had been. She explained, "There is a reason for that. You are in The Hague in Holland, where all the national embassies are located. Your wife checked that you are a 'minister from the United States.' We thought that meant you were an ambassador working for President George Bush. Everyone wanted to meet the ambassador from America who was staying in our hospital." She was explaining my apparent mistaken identity. Smiling, I replied, "As a matter of fact, I *am* an ambassador for Christ. I represent the King."

As I was being checked out, the nurse gave me a prescription and said that I would have to take these drugs for the rest of my life. I said, "I am not too keen on taking medicine." She indicated that because I had a heart attack, it was important to take the medication regularly. I thought, "I am not going to receive that report. My God is bigger than that, and my heart is going to return to normal."

My Dream

After I returned home, I continued thinking about what happened in Holland. I had always been concerned about the health of the body of Christ. That was why I started Healing Rooms Ministries. Though the ministry was growing, I was asking the Holy Spirit why we were not making more progress in getting people healed. It seemed that people were as sick as ever.

We were seeing an increase in healings, and at the same time it seemed there was also an increase in sickness in the church. I became aware that not only was I seeing this problem in others, but it was also the problem I was experiencing in my own health. I was overweight, out of shape, and unhealthy. I knew there was an answer to this overwhelming problem and that God had the answer.

Then one night I had a dream. It was simple; in the dream I became strong. That is all it was. There were no details; I had simply become strong. The next morning I told Michelle, "I had this strange dream in which I became strong. And when I got up this morning, I even *felt* stronger." It was like this dream was imprinted in my spirit, and I knew I was going to become strong. I did not have a clue how that could happen for me. I had never exercised, except maybe doing jumping jacks in my high school PE class. I thought, "I am in my sixties. It's a little late for that."

So I said to Michelle, "I will give this dream a month to see what it means." After a week or two of no apparent answer, I asked God, "How are you going to make me strong?" He said, "I am not going to make you strong; you are going to make yourself strong." I asked, "I am? How can that happen?" He said, "You will have to lift weights." I groaned, "You mean heavy things?" That divine encounter began a long, life-changing conversation with God.

"Do you know how old I am? I am sixty-four years old," I explained, as though God did not know my age. God said, "I have done some amazing things with old people." I remembered Moses leading the children of Israel out of bondage when he was eighty and Caleb asking for a mountain when he was also eighty years old, to mention a few. Let me suggest that you never argue with God; you will not win.

So now I was feeling a little bit of trauma. I could not imagine myself lifting weights at my age; that seemed insane. While I continued complaining, what did God do? I was watching the news on TV, which was airing a report on a mayor of a large city in Canada. She was in her mideighties and running for her sixth or seventh term as mayor. The city had become debt free under her leadership. The reporter asked her, "What do you do for recreation?" He had my attention. She said, "I play ice hockey." Feeling that God must be smiling, I said, "God, that was not fair." But I heard it. I stopped complaining and began my search on how to become strong.

Becoming Strong

I searched the Internet for exercise programs and exercise equipment. When Michelle would take me shopping, I would stop at sporting goods stores and inquire about exercise equipment. I had this spiritual deposit within me of the dream in which I had become strong, and it was not going away. In my research I discovered some interesting facts about health:

- Your age does not determine your health.

- Every hour of exercise will add days to your life expectancy.[2]

I thought, "Wow, I can serve God ten years more with strength and health." I even told my staff on my sixty-fifth birthday, "I am going to reverse time and start getting younger." After all, the Bible says, "For as he thinks within himself, so he is" (Prov. 23:7). I thought, "I am changing my thinking. I am not going to get old and fall apart. I can change the way I eat and begin to exercise and transform my body. I want to run the race to the finish with strength."

I was determined get some exercise equipment to help me in my quest to become strong. One day, while we were on our way to the mall, we passed a sporting goods store that had a banner hanging out front: "Going out of business." I said to Michelle, "Let's stop and see if they have any exercise equipment." I thought maybe I could get a good deal. We entered the store, and there was a stack cable machine with a seat on it; it was the kind that offered opportunity to do full-body exercises with it.

I asked the salesman if he had any more of these machines in stock. He said that was the only one left and the price was reduced by 50 percent. I said, "I will take it. Can you put it in the back of our SUV?" So I purchased it. Two men placed the box on a cart and loaded the machine into our SUV. On our way home I was telling Michelle the good deal we got and how this machine would make me strong. I was excited about beginning an exercise program on my new machine. Michelle said I should set it up in our basement. I agreed.

We pulled into our driveway on the ground level of our home, and Michelle got out of the car and said, "Have fun." Then she left me there and went into the house. I got out of the car and opened the tailgate to remove my new machine. I could not even remove the lid on the box it was in. I had to get a box cutter and painstakingly cut the box apart so that I could see the contents.

Then I discovered I did not have enough strength to carry more than a few pieces at a time down the stairs to the basement. How could there be so many heavy things in one box? Six hours later I finally had this thing put together. I could hardly get back up the stairs to tell Michelle I had finally finished assembling my new machine.

Exhausted, I thought, "This machine has almost killed me, and I haven't even gotten started with exercise."

No Pain—No Gain

I began to exercise, using the chart that came with the machine. Let me tell you, my flesh went into immediate rebellion. It began to talk to me: "What are you trying to do, kill me?" I felt pain in places where a body should never feel pain. Muscles that had lain dormant for years suddenly started waking up. And there was a war going on between my spirit, mind, and flesh. My spirit wanted to reach the goal of becoming strong; my flesh was begging me to quit this senseless, painful activity. I was determined to win this war.

I realized that I had spent a lifetime with my mind in charge of feeding my flesh whatever it wanted—food, inactivity, rest. Both my mind and flesh were happy in that lifestyle. But since God had given me that dream of becoming strong, my spirit had taken control and was telling my mind what to feed my flesh. My mind did not want to listen. And my flesh did not want to obey. I was very aware that I had become conformed to the world's order of things in the matter of food and lack of exercise. Now I realized that my mind had to be renewed so that it would obey God's will regarding how I eat and exercise.

I kept pressing forward, against my natural desires, to exercise three days a week. After the initial "trauma" to my mind and body, something amazing began to happen: *I began to get stronger.* I realized that I could walk up stairs without feeling stress to my legs. I did not have to push with my arms to get up from a chair. What really surprised me was that as my body became stronger, so did my spirit.

I experienced a confidence I did not have before I began to exercise. I began to feel younger. Instead of complaining, it was as though my body was thanking my spirit for pursuing its dream to become strong. Before I started exercising regularly, *gravity* was my enemy; now it was becoming my friend. In the beginning, the resistance that gravity gave to the weights was painful to my flesh. Because of my weakness, lifting weights against gravity required a lot of effort and made me sore. My flesh did not want to work out; it wanted the easy route that let me do only what "feels good." But it was too late to give in to my flesh. I realized that this mentality was what triggered the failure of my health, causing a heart attack. And I had a dream.

Learning the Power of Resistance

All success requires plans and actions. Without a specific plan and corresponding actions for its success, you bring poverty to every area of your life—poverty in relationships, finances, health, and ultimately in your spiritual life. The writer of the Proverbs confirms this sad reality:

> How long will you lie down, O sluggard? When will you arise from your sleep? "A little sleep, a little slumber, a little folding of the hands to rest"—your poverty will come in like a vagabond and your need like an armed man.
>
> —PROVERBS 6:9–11

> Poverty and shame will come to him who neglects discipline, but he who regards reproof will be honored.
>
> —PROVERBS 13:18

> The sluggard buries his hand in the dish, but will not even bring it back to his mouth.
>
> —PROVERBS 19:24

According to the Scriptures, time alone will bring poverty because poverty requires nothing of you. The flesh is so naturally lazy that, according to the proverb, in its extreme it will not even feed itself. As I accepted the reproof of the Lord against my lazy flesh and pursued the discipline of exercise, I overcame my "poverty" of health and achieved the success I pursued.

I discovered that it is the power of resistance that makes you strong, both physically and spiritually. *Resistance* can be defined as opposition. It is when you overcome opposition that you will increase in strength. You cannot be an overcomer, physically or spiritually, unless you have something you need to overcome and you persist until you do so.

When you lift weights to become stronger, the greater the resistance, the stronger you become. Without that resistance, developing strength is not possible. It is not anything inherent in the weights themselves that make you strong; it is what you do with them that results in strengthening you. As a matter of fact, if you dropped one of them on your big toe, it would make you decidedly weaker.

I found that as I overcame the resistance of each ten-pound weight in my exercise program, I grew in physical strength; I could then add more weight resistance to increase my strength. In the beginning of my program I thought I would never lift that one-hundred-pound stack; now I do it easily.

Spiritual resistance

The Holy Spirit taught me a great lesson as I consistently used the weight machine to create resistance so that I could become physically stronger. He spoke the words of Jesus to me: "In the world you have tribulation [resistance], but take courage; I have overcome the world" (John 16:33). Then He said to me, "Your ability to overcome will determine your strength, which gives you success." I began to understand other Bible passages in a new way as well that teach us to war against—to resist—the flesh and the devil:

> Submit therefore to God. *Resist* the devil and he will flee from you.
>
> —JAMES 4:7, EMPHASIS ADDED

Your spiritual strength to resist the evil one comes from your submission to God. In other words, you cannot overcome his plans for your destruction in your own strength. You have to partner with God in order to receive His strength to push through and overcome the resistance of your mind and flesh, as well as the wiles of the enemy who continually works for your demise (John 10:10).

Your failure or success in every area of life will be determined by your understanding of overcoming resistance. You can experience failure because of the resistance of the enemy, or you can enjoy success by drawing near to God and receiving His strength to resist the enemy. The key is, are you resisting the enemy, or is he resisting you? The one who does the resisting is the one who has the power to win. When you resist him in the power of God, you will always win.

The apostle Paul exhorted believers:

> Finally, be strong in the Lord and in the strength of His might.
> —EPHESIANS 6:10

The word *strong* means "to be empowered, enabled, to make strong"[3] so that you can overcome evil by putting on the whole armor of God (Eph. 6:11–17). The apostle Peter also commanded that we resist the evil one: "But resist him, firm in your faith" (1 Pet. 5:9). The Greek word for *resist* means "to oppose, to set oneself against, to withstand."[4]

"Resisting" age through proper exercise

In physical exercise you do not increase the resistance (weight) until you are strong enough to handle the resistance you are currently using. Without consistently developing your physical strength, gravity becomes your enemy when you get older; you do not have the strength to resist its effects on your body. Developing strength through resistance gives you energy and allows you to counter the effects of gravity at any age. I realized early on that to have a strong body meant that I needed to do cardio and strength exercises. I understood the value of cardio exercise for heart health, for increasing stamina, and for general health.

But as we get older, we need strength exercises as well to resist the aging process. With age there is a tendency to slow down and not exercise as much, which triggers a vicious cycle of deterioration. Because we are not as active, we gain weight; the added weight and the deterioration of muscle put more pressure on our joints. This causes joint failure that results in the need for knee and hip replacements. In addition, other health issues can begin to take hold, such as arthritis and general pain. God made our bodies so that our strong muscles would support our joints. This healthy muscle support allows the joints to remain healthy, no matter what age we are.

My father and two older brothers had knee problems. I noticed, as I got older and gained weight through poor nutrition, that my knee joints also became sore and painful. It became difficult to walk up stairs. I was experiencing the joint deterioration cycle I just described. However, I thought my joint problem was hereditary, that because my father and brothers had this problem, I was destined to have it also. I thought that the "generational curse" of bad knees was going to prevent me from achieving good health.

Here is an example of the value of partnering with the Holy Spirit to achieve good health. I mentioned earlier that wonderful promise in Galatians 3:13:

> Christ redeemed us from the curse of the Law, having become a curse for us—for it is written, "Cursed is everyone who hangs on a tree."

Then the Holy Spirit spoke to my heart: "You have been redeemed from the curse of bad knees." And He reminded me of the promise, "Greater is He who is in you than he who is in the world" (1 John 4:4). I understood that He who is in me did not want me to have bad knees.

When I first began my workout, my knees began to hurt so bad I thought the pain would stop me. I would apply the "medicine" of the Word to the pain and continue to work out. I would hear the Holy Spirit declaring the words of the prophet Isaiah: "Surely He has borne our griefs (sicknesses, weaknesses, and distresses) and carried our sorrows and pains..." (Isa. 53:4, AMP).

After a while, the pain left my knees and never returned. My improved nutrition and exercise workout with the medicine of the Word restored my knees to health. I have been redeemed from the curse of knee pain; therefore I do not have to carry that pain from which I have been redeemed.

Through the process of overcoming joint pain, I experienced a good kind of pain: muscle pain. It was only temporary. We have all heard of growing pains that children experience. Well, older people can experience pain as they "grow" muscle that has deteriorated over the years. It goes back to the old saying I mentioned, "no pain—no gain." When I experienced the muscle pain, I knew it meant that old, ignored, deteriorating muscles were coming to life and growing. As I continued my exercise regimen, I eventually overcame all pain in my body.

Meet Mr. Universe

So, here I was, having a dream that I became strong, beginning to exercise, and realizing that I desperately needed to change my diet. I was sixty-four years old and had never known anyone who was a trainer, weight lifter, or dietitian. So what was the chance that after my dream and my decision to become strong was in progress, Mr. Universe would come to my home four months later?

It happened. Mr. Ron Williams, the most decorated natural bodybuilder in the world, came to my house and told me he felt God sent him to me to be my personal trainer. That got my attention! His titles include seven-time winner of Mr. Natural Universe and Mr. Natural

Olympia and six-time winner of Mr. Natural World. He is a professor of exercise physiology and nutrition.[5]

Ron and his wife, Tonja, are called by God to help God's people lose fat and become healthy. They began to help Michelle and me with our diet and exercise programs. We read his book, *Faith and Fat Loss*,[6] which helped us to lose fat through a daily thirty-minute fat loss program. We learned to eat nutritional food six times a day. Ron said that our intake of food needs to be like wood you put on a fire continually to keep the fire (our metabolism) burning evenly day and night.

I discovered that the food I was eating was not helping my metabolism create energy; it was only going to storage in the fat cells of my body. Ron taught me how to do my workouts to get the maximum results and to take pressure off my joints while lifting weights. I was able to build muscle around my joints without putting pressure on them in the process so that they could become healthy.

As a result of their instruction and help, Michelle and I began to lose weight and become strong. I reduced my weight from 233 pounds to 195 pounds. I could now do things with ease that I could not do before. I went back to my cardiologist for a checkup. After reading the results of the test, he sent me a letter saying my heart was normal. As a matter of fact, he said he could not even tell that I had suffered a heart attack.

My Staff Noticed

As Michelle and I pursued physical health and began to lose weight, our staff took notice. It was as though our pursuit of strength became contagious. Everyone seemed to show interest in getting into shape. I told them, "If you are interested in losing weight and getting into shape, I will shorten your workday by thirty minutes three days a week, with pay, so that we can all participate in a thirty-minute 'Ron Williams fat loss workout.'"

I invited Ron and Tonja Williams to come to our training center and show my staff how to do the fat loss program. There we were, some of us over fifty years old, doing a thirty-minute cardio workout without a rest period. We were used to rest—continually. Talk about trauma. What, no coffee break! No entertainment? Speaking of entertainment, we became the entertainment, with our groans and huffing and puffing, laughing to keep from crying.

But we kept doing the program, and gradually it got easier. As it got easier, we began to see positive changes in each other. We all got thinner and stronger. We began to follow the prescribed diet of combining carbs and proteins. We put good fuel in our bodies, as we did the workout and were seeing results. What had not been much fun in the beginning became fun later on as we worked out together and encouraged each other toward our goals.

Everyone set their own pace based on where they began the challenge physically. Through this process, our staff combined for hundreds of pounds of weight loss, and we became stronger. I saw this company-wide program as an investment in our ministry. In this way, my staff could invest in their own lives to become healthy. A healthy staff makes a valuable investment into the ministry. A healthy staff with a strong immune system will not allow sickness to get a foothold; this results in less sick days in the ministry.

People who are healthy and strong are more successful in reaching their daily goals. The added energy this thirty-minute workout gave us became the driving force that sustained us in our pursuit of health. The power that became our fuel was the godly desire to have a healthy body in which the Holy Spirit could dwell unhindered in fulfilling His will in our lives. His love for us makes all things possible.

A New Facet to Our Healing Ministry

Michelle and I began to incorporate this health message, with our testimonies, into our healing conferences. I cannot tell you how many people would come up to us after the messages on health with tears in their eyes to thank us. They told us how they struggled with weight problems and physical issues, and no one in the church seemed to provide a kingdom answer that would help them overcome their health issues. Here is an e-mail we received from a grateful believer:

> We read your article on health and healing. We were interested in the section where you said, "Our Age Does Not Determine Our Health." We are entering our sixth year as missionaries. I am sixty-eight years old, and my wife is sixty-six years old. We are both overweight, and we realize that our weight is causing some problems with energy and getting around. We need to be able to move and go places and do things for God. We both need help with better nutrition and to lose weight. We don't have the energy to do each day what God has called us to. It captured our interest when you said your energy level was better than it has been in twenty years. We would appreciate any help you can give us.

This e-mail speaks volumes to the overwhelming need in the body of Christ to be healthy in order to run the race that God has ordained for us with strength:

> Let us run with endurance the race that is set before us.
> —HEBREWS 12:1

The Greek word for *endurance* means "a characteristic of a man who is not swerved from his deliberate purpose, but patiently, constantly, endures trials, persevering to succeed with strength."[7] The couple who wrote this e-mail realized that being out of shape had become a hindrance to the work God called them to complete with strength. Another friend wrote:

Thank you for your teaching on healing and health. Someone needed to remind us that being healthy means we have to do our part. Oftentimes people want God to heal them of things they brought on themselves by misuse of the temple He has given us. I want to live to one hundred, and every one of those years to be used by God completely. To give Him less years than He planned for me to have to serve Him is a crime.

Wow! This believer lays it out for us. First, we need to do our part. Second, we can live to one hundred and beyond by pursuing good health. Third, it would be a crime to allow our years to be stolen from His kingdom purposes. The Word of God asks the poignant question: "Why should you die before your time?" (Eccles. 7:17). It also promises long life to those who keep God's commandments: "Let your heart keep my commandments; for length of days and years of life and peace they will add to you" (Prov. 3:1–2).

Remember, failure requires a decision backed up by no effort. Though the statement "no pain—no gain" may be a cliché, it is true. While it takes little or no effort to deteriorate physically along with millions of people who have adopted our American lifestyle of "indulgence of the flesh," as believers we are accountable to a different standard of life. We must allow our minds to be transformed by the Word of God and choose to be a suitable temple for the Spirit of God, who dwells in us. He will give us the grace and wisdom to overcome every obstacle as we build up our spirit man with the Word of God. Understanding that it is God's will for believers, His church, to prosper and be in health as our soul (mind, will, emotions) prospers (3 John 2) is imperative if we are to fulfill the destiny to which He has called us.

Chapter 3

GOD'S WILL FOR HIS BODY

God calls His Word seed because it
has fulfillment within it.

To understand God's will for His children to live in health, we must go back to the beginning when God created mankind and revealed His purpose for them. It is also important to know that God has never changed His original purpose as revealed throughout the Scriptures, from Genesis through Revelation. In Genesis we read:

> "Let Us make man in Our image, according to Our likeness; and let them rule over the fish of the sea and over the birds of the sky and over the cattle and over all the earth, and over every creeping thing that creeps on the earth."...and God said to them, "Be fruitful and multiply, and fill the earth, and *subdue* it."
> —GENESIS 1:26, 28, EMPHASIS ADDED

God created mankind in His image and likeness and gave him the power of dominion, or rulership, over all the earth. We do not know how long this first couple walked and talked with God, living in unbroken fellowship with Him, as He intended. But we do know that they communed with Him as He walked in the garden in the cool of the day (Gen. 3:8). Created in the likeness of God meant, for one thing, that there was no sickness in that paradise, because there is no sickness in God.

God's goal for mankind was to live in perfect fellowship with Him and to rule the earth that God created for them to tend and enjoy. Yet God and man could not live in divine communion if man was only a "puppet"; God gave him free will to choose to love God and to walk in fellowship with Him. That relationship of love required that mankind choose to obey God's commands, given for his well-being— wholeness, health.

The only way that man could become *unhealthy* was to rebel against God in disobedience, which God calls sin. When Adam chose to disobey God's command not to eat of the tree of the knowledge of good and evil, he lost his authority, his dominion over God's kingdom on the earth. Originally, Scripture indicates that mankind had remarkable longevity. Yet, because of the Fall, God reduced man's life to 120 years (Gen. 6:3). When Adam lost the authority that God gave him, the devil gained authority over Adam. Through sin, sickness and death entered into the life of mankind.

Hundreds of years later, when the psalmist referred to the days of our lives containing seventy or eighty years (Ps. 90:10), he was reflecting on the sad reality he observed, based on lives that suffered under the sinfulness of mankind after the Fall. I believe that when we embrace a kingdom lifestyle, we can return to God's mandate for mankind to live 120 years of a quality life. It is interesting that medical science is now conducting studies that confirm this possibility, citing that half the population could live to the age of 120 years, given certain environmental and medical criteria.[1] Have they discovered the "natural elements" that God initiated when He mandated a man's lifespan to be 120 years?

> Then the LORD said, "My Spirit shall not strive with man forever, because he also is flesh; nevertheless his days shall be one hundred and twenty years."
>
> —GENESIS 6:3

It is interesting to note here that the word *flesh* simply means "of the body of humans or animals, the body itself, nakedness."[2] The flesh is not evil; it has no nature of its own. According to the apostle Paul, "The mind *set on the flesh* [body³] is death, but the mind set on the Spirit is life and peace" (Rom. 8:6, emphasis added). Then he declares: "However, you are not in the flesh but in the Spirit, if indeed the Spirit of God dwells in you" (v. 9).

Later Paul exhorts believers to "be transformed by the renewing of your mind, so that you may prove what the will of God is…" (Rom. 12:2). The believer's renewed mind will set itself on the things of God, how to fulfill His will and walk in destiny. Adam, in the beginning, was living in the image and likeness of God with full dominion over all of life, fulfilling his destiny to rule the earth. Then he disobeyed God and was no longer like God. Adam became selfish, and as a result, he subjected all of mankind to the law of sin and death.

According to God's mandate, mankind would become restricted to 120 years of life. What is important is to know that God has given us the potential of 120 years of life. If God has given us 120 years of potential life, should we not be able to achieve it? Yes. I believe we can, as we embrace the power of His redemption and walk in stewardship of His temple.

The Truth of Redemption Sets Us Free

The New Testament teaches that Christ became the "last Adam" when He came to the earth to redeem us, bringing healing of body, mind, and spirit to those who believe in Him. He came to set us free from sin and sickness, as we mentioned was the fulfillment of Isaiah's prophecy (Isaiah 53), as well as many others.

Redemption through Christ, who came to fulfill the law (Matt. 5:17), sets us free from the curse of the Law (Gal. 3:13) and places us into the supernatural grace of God:

For sin shall not be master over you, for you are not under law but under grace.

—ROMANS 6:14

We need to walk in that fulfillment, applying God's wonderful grace to our lives. Grace is not a power God gives us so that we can bear up under sin and sickness. Grace is the power of God in us to destroy sin and sickness from which Jesus died to redeem us:

The Son of God appeared for this purpose, to destroy the works of the devil.

—1 JOHN 3:8

Because of Christ's sacrifice, when we accept Him as our Savior, we are baptized into the body of Christ (1 Cor. 12:13) by the same Holy Spirit that raised Christ from the dead:

But if the Spirit of Him who raised Jesus from the dead dwells in you, He who raised Christ Jesus from the dead will also give life to your mortal bodies through His Spirit who dwells in you.

—ROMANS 8:11

This promise guarantees our healing and deliverance from sickness. Too many Christians justify why the enemy has made them sick rather than embracing the truth that Jesus has made them well. The Holy Spirit dwelling in us is giving life to our mortal bodies, and Scripture says, "Greater is He who is in you than he who is in the world" (1 John 4:4). When we are born again as believers in Christ, we have a greater power inside us than our enemy who comes against us. When we receive Christ's redemption, He returns our authority to us that Adam had before he sinned; we can walk free from the curse of sin and sickness from which we have been redeemed.

On the cross Jesus "bought up" sin and sickness. He paid our ransom to set us free from the curse of sin and sickness. If He paid for it, why should we? Yet, because we still have free will, we must *choose* to receive the grace that God gives us to live without sin and sickness. When we make that choice, God gives us His authority, His power in us that allows us to walk in victory.

Redemption through repentance

I mentioned that redemption is *positional* for a believer. That is, it is a position you choose when you are reconciled to God. You enter this blessed position through repentance. When you repent of your sin and accept Christ as your Savior, you are redeemed *from* the penalty of sin. The meaning of the Greek word for *repent* (*metanoia*[4]) "involves a turning with contrition from sin to God; the repentant sinner is in the proper condition to accept the divine forgiveness."[5]

Repentance is the avenue God uses to redeem you and place you back into His divine purpose for you, the same purpose He gave to Adam in the beginning. As redeemed people, we are the righteousness of Christ (2 Cor. 5:21). The Greek word for *righteousness* means "right standing or alignment to God; the condition acceptable to God."[6]

In this redeemed position where we stand, no weapon formed against us prospers (Isa. 54:17). It is a place where we can walk without sin and enjoy divine health. We are no longer walking as people who are conformed to the world; we are allowing our mind to be renewed to a kingdom mentality. Our mind now agrees with the Word of God: "I do not have to bear this sickness because Jesus bore it for me, as 1 Peter 2:24 states. I am now set free from the law of sin and death because I have been redeemed from it."

> For the law of the Spirit of life in Christ Jesus has set you free from the law of sin and of death.
>
> —ROMANS 8:2

Many believers accept negative things in their lives that they do not have to because they do not recognize the authority they have in their redeemed position in Christ. If the postman comes to your front door with a special delivery package with your name on it, and you hear a bunch of hissing and rattling inside it, are you going to accept the package? No. Return it to sender. In that same way, spiritually you do not have to accept any sin or sickness from which you have been redeemed, even if it seems to find "your address."

God's Word declares, "My people are destroyed for lack of knowledge" (Hos. 4:6). It is what we *know* that determines where we go. Understanding our heavenly position in Christ (Col. 3:1) should dictate the quality of our lives on this earth. We must not measure heaven by the sinful condition of the earth; the condition of our earth must be changed by heaven as we choose to walk in the fullness of Christ's redemption.

You Are a New Creature

Through redemption, you have become a new creation:

> Therefore if anyone is in Christ, he is a new creation; old things have passed away; behold, all things have become new.
> —2 Corinthians 5:17, nkjv

As a new creation, you can walk in health because redemption has placed you "in Christ" and you are complete in Him:

> For in Him *all* the fullness of the Deity dwells in bodily form, and in Him you have been made *complete*, and He is the head over all rule and authority.
> —Colossians 2:9–10, emphasis added

We have been made complete in Christ. According to the Greek, to be *complete* means "to cram, level up to the brim, to finish, to fulfill, to render perfect."[7] God is telling us, as members of the body of

Christ, that we have everything we need to walk in wholeness, which includes physical health. Our potential is that the life of Christ can impact our mortal bodies as well as our spirit and soul. What Jesus provided wasn't only for the spirit of man, but it would also give life to the whole man: spirit, mind, and body. I believe health is part of this wonderful redemption.

The Colossian church began to adopt pagan philosophies and practices as part of their Christian culture. The apostle Paul warned them, "Let no one keep defrauding you of your prize" through these exalted "fleshly" ideas (Col. 2:18). In that same way, when we allow the things of the world to influence our thinking, we lose our wonderful prize of completeness that is available to us in Christ. Too many people cannot walk in the freedom that God desires because they submit themselves willingly to the bondages the enemy wants them to embrace. Paul asked the Colossians this important question:

> If you have died with Christ to the elementary principles of the world, why, as if you were living in the world, do you submit yourself to decrees [of the world]?
>
> —COLOSSIANS 2:20

Today, as redeemed people, we cannot conform to our godless culture without defrauding ourselves of the blessings of health and life God has available for us. The apostle Paul, as I mentioned, urged believers to "not be conformed to this world, but be transformed by the renewing of your mind" (Rom. 12:2). I hear so many Christians say, "I just can't believe that we can walk in health because I see so many of my family and friends sick." Jesus said that it is the truth of God that sets us free (John 8:32). The truth is that God wants you to be healthy; the devil wants you to be sick.

Yet your belief system will be formed according to where you focus your mind. If you focus on the circumstances around you, the condition of your family and friends, you will have difficulty believing the truth of God's Word, that it is possible to walk in health. The truth is, the Word of God is not determined by the condition of man; the condition of man is changed by the power of God's Word. You do not have to bring about wholeness in your own strength; the Word declares you have already been made complete in Christ (Col. 2:10). Now you must choose to focus on the truth and walk in what has already been provided. You cannot receive what you do not believe.

The reason we are complete in Christ is that when we are redeemed, we become a new creation (2 Cor. 5:17), as I mentioned earlier. The Greek word for *creation* means "an act of founding, establishing, original formation."[8] When you repent of your sins and accept Christ as your Savior, you are restored to the original formation or position mankind enjoyed with God before Adam fell to sin. You can begin to move forward in life as a new creature in Christ, as Paul declared: "The old things passed away; behold, new things have come" (v. 17).

What are the old things that have passed away? They include everything that belongs to the curse of sin from which you have been redeemed. God is saying not to hold on to old things such as poverty, sickness, and death. You have authority over them now. New things are available to you as a new creation in Christ. What are the new things that you now have at your disposal? The apostle Paul concludes that those new things include our becoming "the righteousness of God in Him" (v. 21).

I don't know about you, but I have decided that if it is not part of the righteousness of God, I am not taking it. Too many Christians are still hanging on to the old things. Sickness is one of those old things; it falls under the curse of sin and death. As a new creation in Christ, you are to only receive the new things that are from God. There is no sickness in God. Jesus came to destroy the works of the devil, which includes sickness (1 John 3:8). You can receive this "new thing" from God to walk in health and be free from sickness.

In the meaning of *creation* there is also the idea of the proprietorship of the manufacturer.[9] In other words, God is our Maker, or *manufacturer*. When we become a new creation, He moves in to set up His proprietorship—His kingdom business. The Holy Spirit dwells in you for the fulfillment of the will of God on the earth. That is what Paul meant when he declared, "I have been crucified with Christ; and it is no longer I who live, but Christ lives in me; and the life which I now live in the flesh I live by faith in the Son of God who loved me and gave Himself up for me" (Gal. 2:20).

The body of Christ is referred to as God's "household" in the Scriptures; He wants to set up His kingdom business in us. Christ is the cornerstone of this supernatural building of God in the earth.

> So then you are no longer stranger and aliens, but you are fellow citizens with the saints, and are of *God's household*, having been built upon the foundation of the apostles and prophets, Christ Jesus Himself being the corner stone, in whom the whole building, being fitted together, is growing into *a holy temple* in the Lord, in whom you also are being built together into a *dwelling* of God in the Spirit.
> —EPHESIANS 2:19–21, EMPHASIS ADDED

As a new creation, you become the dwelling place of God in the Spirit. And "where the Spirit of the Lord is, there is liberty" (2 Cor. 3:17). You can enter into freedom because it is not what you do but what God is doing through you. He gives you His Word, His Spirit, His armor, His anointing, and His life so that your life will prosper. He only desires to have your will so that His will can be done through you. When this happens, you become a holy temple, a place where God conducts His kingdom business on the earth. As a Christian, your responsibility is to be a good steward of His temple.

> Do you not know that you are a temple of God, and that the
> Spirit of God dwells in you? If any man *destroys* the temple of
> God, God will *destroy* him, for the temple of God is holy, and
> that is what you are.
>
> —1 CORINTHIANS 3:16–17, EMPHASIS ADDED

We must understand what God is saying when telling us we are His temple, occupied by the Spirit of God. He warns us not to destroy the temple of God. The word *destroy* in this passage means "to defile, to spoil, waste or to ruin."[10] It is referring to a believer, a person, who is the house of God. In essence, God is saying, "If you ruin My house, I will ruin you." I believe He is referring to our responsibility of stewardship of our bodies, which are the temples of the Spirit of God.

Because the word *destroy* is the same Greek word in both instances in verse 17, it could be translated like this: "If anyone *ruins* the temple of God, God will *ruin* him." I wondered, "If we ruin ourselves, then why would God need to ruin us?" I believe what God is saying is that if we make the decision to ruin His temple, our body, with unhealthy life-style choices, He will agree with our decisions. He may not agree with what we are doing, but because He gave us free will that allows us to choose, He cannot break that covenant and override our choices. When we make a decision outside of the will of God, God honors our decision, though His will cannot be fulfilled in us as a result of our poor choice.

Sometimes we make lifestyle decisions that harm our body, His temple, and then wonder why God does not intervene. We need to be reminded of God's eternal covenant with Israel that applies to us as well: "I call heaven and earth to witness against you today, that I have set before you life and death, the blessing and the curse. So choose life in order that you may live, you and your descendants" (Deut. 30:19). Our power of choice, as born-again Christians, remains intact—we must choose life or death regarding stewardship of His temple. I have found that choosing life is less painful.

It is interesting to note here how adamant God is about His temple, not wanting it to be defiled or ruined. He declares that His temple is holy, meaning you are holy, created anew in His righteousness. God does not defile us; we defile ourselves through the poor choices we make. Doesn't it make sense that if you are the dwelling place of God's Spirit, God would want a healthy house? We need to value what God has made available for us and understand what we have within us. Jesus said:

> For behold, the kingdom of God is in your midst.
>
> —LUKE 17:21

The value of any house lies in what it contains. In the world, when you have wealth, you want to secure it. There are thieves who want to steal your worldly wealth. If you own gold bars, you probably do not store them in a cardboard box in your house. You store them in a secure vault so that thieves cannot get to them. In a similar manner, God deposits great, supernatural wealth inside of us: Himself. The enemy wants to steal that spiritual wealth. He works to convince you to break down the cardboard box—your "earthen vessel" (2 Cor. 4:7). If he succeeds, you could lose the treasure inside. But if you align yourself and your choices with what God puts inside of you, that divine treasure will help you to strengthen your earthen vessel.

The Atonement

Learning to appreciate the value of the divine treasure within you will motivate you to care for your body as the temple of God. Christ's atonement for you makes it possible to be restored to His will for your prosperity in every area of life. The word *atonement* carries the idea of "covering," "purging," and "pardon."[11] *To atone* also means to reconcile or to appease or satisfy a debt. As our Redeemer, Jesus became our substitute in death to atone for our sin and our sickness. Through redemption Jesus bought up our sin and sickness. As I mentioned earlier, the prophet Isaiah declares this reality:

> Surely He has borne our griefs (*sicknesses, weaknesses, and distresses*) and carried our *sorrows and pain*....He was wounded for our transgressions, He was bruised for our guilt and iniquities; the chastisement [needful to obtain] peace and well-being for us was upon Him, and with the stripes [that wounded] Him we are healed and made whole.
>
> —ISAIAH 53:4–5, AMP, EMPHASIS ADDED

Jesus bore our sickness in His death on the cross; He carried our pain so that by His stripes we would be healed. As I mentioned, the word *healed* means "cured, restored, made whole."[12] We are made whole because the blood of Jesus has cleansed us from all unrighteousness (1 John 1:9). I believe one of the most revelatory words in the Bible is the word *all*. When God says *all*, I believe He means *all*. By the blood of Jesus shed on the cross, God has cleansed us from *all* of the curse. Isaiah's prophetic word is in the past tense: He *bore*, He *carried*, our sickness and pain on the cross; it has already been done.

Christ bore our sin and sickness on the cross so that we would not have to bear them. By His stripes we have been healed. Now we can be whole, because sickness no longer has authority over us; we are cleansed from it. Health is available to us. But because God gave us free will, just as we have to choose to accept Christ as Savior, we also have to choose to steward our bodies into health.

Health is not an automatic blessing to a believer because we have an enemy who wants to steal our health. And our fleshly desires often go against the requirements for good health. I have found that I have to work hard to maintain my health. When I ease up, things begin to go the other way. The important thing is that as we submit to God's power working in us, we can reign in life over everything that would defeat us:

> For if by the transgression of the one, death reigned through the one, *much more* those who receive the abundance of grace and of the gift of righteousness will reign in life through the One, Jesus Christ.
>
> —ROMANS 5:17, EMPHASIS ADDED

When you are reigning in life, you are ruling from a foundation of divine power. That foundation of power in Christ is the Holy Spirit. The truth of this verse is powerful: because one man sinned, death reigned over all humanity. And because Jesus Christ became our atonement for sin, when we receive His grace and righteousness, *much more* we will reign in life. That means if sickness once reigned over you, now, through Jesus Christ, you can reign over sickness and walk in abundant health.

It is very difficult for some people to believe God's promise that "No weapon that is formed against you will prosper..." (Isa. 54:17). Yet that is the truth of God's Word. You must believe His Word in order to reign in life. The Scriptures tell you to arm yourself with the "shield of faith with which you will be able to extinguish *all* the flaming missiles of the evil one" (Eph. 6:16, emphasis added). You can reign in life now because the power to overcome is God's and not yours.

A Quickened Body

When I first began this journey of discovery to obtain health, I had difficulty believing it was possible. I could not believe because I had no foundation of truth upon which to rest my faith. As I studied the Scriptures, the Holy Spirit began to bring revelation of these truths to me. Scriptures that I had studied before began to open my understanding to things that I had not seen. All my life I had presented my questions to God; now God began to question me about His Word. One of these scriptures He brought to my attention reads:

> But if the Spirit of him that raised up Jesus from the dead dwell in you, he that raised up Christ from the dead shall also quicken your mortal bodies by his Spirit that dwelleth in you.
>
> —ROMANS 8:11, KJV

I thought I understood this verse, using it as a promise for healing because I was directing a healing ministry. Now the Holy Spirit began to question that partial understanding. He said that this verse is a *health* scripture; it is *positional* in that it speaks to a continuous state of being healed. The same Holy Spirit who raised Jesus from the dead *dwells* in us to give life to our mortal bodies. He doesn't come to visit from time to time. When the scripture says He dwells in us, it means He is in the house on a full-time basis. The same anointing that flows through us to heal the sick is available to maintain our health continually.

Then the verse says that His resurrection power will *quicken* your mortal bodies. That means that His power "arouses and invigorates, giving greater powers of life."[13] To explain, being *quickened* would be like the feeling you get when you stick your finger into a light socket. Your whole body would be quickened by electrical power surging through it. In the natural, if you encounter that kind of power, you need to disconnect quickly or it might kill you. But the Holy Spirit helped me to understand that in the kingdom of God, if you will leave your finger in that *quickening* power, it will give you sustaining life and overcoming power.

I had underestimated the intensity of that quickening power of the Spirit of God, thinking it simply referred to His work in us to keep us alive. Redemption is not given to us to just keep us alive. It is given to us to have the quickening power of God flowing through us to overwhelmingly conquer sin and sickness (Rom. 8:37). In other words, on a full-time basis we have resurrection power quickening our physical bodies, empowering us to reign in life.

Conformed to His Image

Before I understood the power of redemption to position us before God as if we had never sinned, I always carried a sin consciousness in my soul. I felt condemned because of the sin consciousness I carried. This sense of condemnation kept me from living in victory, causing a victim mentality to rule my mind. My unrenewed mind robbed me of my position in Christ and caused me to live under the curse of the fall of man and be conformed to the world.

As a result, I always justified my *condition*, my unhealed state, rather than declaring my *position* in Christ. I was always explaining why I was not healed, why I was not prospering, and why I had no victory. I did not realize the truth that a born-again Christian is actually transformed into the image and likeness of God by virtue of being a new creation. I could not enjoy the reality that in Christ Jesus there is no longer condemnation from sin consciousness. Then I saw this scripture with new revelation of the Spirit of God:

> Therefore there is now no condemnation for those who are in Christ Jesus.
>
> —ROMANS 8:1

Accepting this truth brought me out of a failure mind-set. In the old mind-set, no matter how hard I had tried, I could not walk in divine health. I only saw myself trying to hang on until the Second Coming of Christ. I felt that whatever happened to my physical body was going to happen, and there was not much I could do about it. Even though I knew, in the beginning, before the Fall, man walked with God in health, I thought, "That was then, this is now, and I am in a mess. If Christ doesn't return soon, I may not make it." My sin consciousness caused me to live in constant fear of getting sick or going broke. Then I read Romans 8:29 with new understanding:

> For those whom He foreknew, He also predestined to become conformed to the image of His Son, so that He would be the first-born among many brethren.

"Wow," I thought, "God knew me ahead of time and predetermined that I would become a new creation. I would be conformed into His image. Now I am in the body of Christ, filled with the Spirit of God. I am in right standing again, cleansed by the blood of Jesus, redeemed from the curse of sin and sickness with resurrection power in me. Now I have the authority to walk in health." Those were transforming thoughts that set me free to believe His promise:

> He who did not spare His own Son, but delivered Him over for us all, how will He not also with Him freely give us all things?
> —ROMANS 8:32

God is telling us that if He gave His best, His only Son, Jesus, why would He not also give us these lesser things such as abundant health? As a matter of fact, Jesus came as the fulfillment of all that is in the will of God for the purpose of conforming us to the image of God.

Healing Is Health

As I have mentioned, I have considered *healing* and *health* as two separate concepts. While that may be true, as I read 3 John 2, I began to understand that both to be healed and to walk in health culminate in wholeness of body, mind, and spirit:

> Beloved, I pray that in all respects you may prosper and be in good health, just as your soul prospers.

In other words, real healing results in health and wholeness. God wants us in all aspects to live our lives in wholeness. Health is His will for us. The Greek word for *salvation, sozo,* means "to make sound or whole, to restore to health."[14] Salvation is to produce wholeness and health in a believer. We are saved by grace to become whole and live continually in a state of health. I was beginning to understand more clearly the words of Jesus:

> For God did not send the Son into the world to judge the world, but that the world might be *saved* through Him.
>
> —JOHN 3:17, EMPHASIS ADDED

Jesus came that we would be made whole in spirit, mind, and body. We may understand how receiving salvation through Christ impacts our spirit and renews our mind, but do we truly understand how it impacts our body? A triune God wants to save a triune man—spirit, soul, and body:

> Now may the God of peace Himself sanctify you entirely; and may your spirit and soul and body be preserved complete, without blame at the coming of our Lord Jesus Christ.
>
> —1 THESSALONIANS 5:23

The apostle Paul prayed for God to sanctify you, or purify you as a holy temple in which the Spirit of God dwells. You are to be purified in spirit, in mind, and in body. This wholeness is only possible as the Holy Spirit occupies a person. As you allow the Holy Spirit to dwell in you, God will preserve you in that position of completeness until Jesus returns.

As members of the body of Christ, we are not separated from Christ, the head of the body. If we are His body and redeemed back into His image and likeness, shouldn't we be like Him when He returns? The Scriptures declare that we are the righteousness of God in Christ (2 Cor. 5:21), and "as He is, so also are we in this world" (1 John 4:17). The body of Christ is to be "the fullness of Him who fills all in all" (Eph. 1:23).

Subduing the flesh

The receptionist at our international offices was telling me about some of the e-mails and phone calls she gets weekly. People call in with a desire to be whole but say things like: "I am too sick to read my Bible." "I am too tired to exercise." Sometimes she hears people say, "I am just too distracted to pray." We have even had people come to us who felt they were too sick to be healed.

The enemy wants to distract you from receiving the promises of God for your wholeness. He does this by afflicting with sickness, mental problems, and weakness. When you are distracted by the enemy, he can establish a stronghold in your life that makes you agree with his lies. That agreement empowers just as agreement in prayer empowers (Matt. 18:19). We have seen people come into the healing rooms so traumatized by their past that they cannot believe they have a future. The enemy works to make a past trauma become a present reality in a believer's life. You need to know that there is safety when you allow the Spirit of God to dwell in you and learn to walk in the Spirit:

> But I say, walk by the Spirit, and you will not carry out the desire of the flesh. For the flesh sets its desire against the Spirit, and the Spirit against the flesh; for these are in opposition to one another, so that you may not do the things that you please. But if you are led by the Spirit, you are not under the Law.
>
> —GALATIANS 5:16–18

The desire of your flesh involves your entire carnal (natural) nature. If you are led by the Spirit, you will not get tripped up by your flesh. The Scriptures teach that your natural nature sets its desire against the Spirit. It is not led by the Spirit but will always follow the world's order that is under the curse of sin. The Holy Spirit quickens you, giving you the power to subdue your flesh under the will of God. The power to live an overcoming life is determined by where you set your mind. The mind set on the Spirit will bring life. When you choose to be led by the Spirit, the Holy Spirit will move, with your will, to defeat your carnal man; in that way you can become whole as a part of the body of Christ. You will not get tripped up if you will walk according to the Spirit of God who dwells in you. A Spirit-led person can walk in health when the flesh is submitted to God.

Our Responsibility

I came to a place where I realized that I had no choice but to consider stewarding my health if I wanted to live. Life and death were set before me when I suffered a heart attack. I chose to live rather than to die from heart disease. The power of God's life within me gave me rulership over my body. I understood that if I was going to walk by the Spirit, I had to obey the Spirit. When I read, "…you are not your own? For you have been bought with a price: therefore glorify God in your body" (1 Cor. 6:19–20), I realized my life belonged to Christ. The problem I had was that I thought I had a life. But the truth is, if the Word says I am not my own, I guess I do not have a life.

The Holy Spirit told me He does not want to travel in a vehicle that is out of shape and broken down. He wants a vehicle that is "driven" by resurrection power. He promised me, "If you begin this journey to health, I will provide the fuel and you can provide the vehicle."

Until then it never occurred to me that when I mistreated my body, subjecting it to bad food and a lack of exercise, I was dishonoring God. To glorify God in your body means to honor Him, living a life filled with His presence. The Holy Spirit showed me that God did not save my body for me to mistreat it; He saved it so that I could take the responsibility to glorify Him in it. I was not born again to have a life; I was born again to have His life. Until I realized this, I was constantly struggling with things in my life that caused conflict. I could not get delivered from things I was hanging on to with my natural man, "my" life.

For example, Michelle and I would go to the grocery store or a restaurant and see a rich food or dessert and say, "I love that." These were the very things we wanted to be delivered from, but we were having a problem getting free from because we had a love relationship with them. It is hard to get delivered from something you love. Yet the things we loved were the very things that caused our physical problems in the first place. Before we could begin our journey to wholeness, we had to change our confession about the things we loved. We had to begin to "love" the foods our bodies needed to be in good health.

You Are What You Say

We realized that if we were going to have our minds renewed to health, we had to think differently. I mentioned earlier that Proverbs 23:7 tells us, "For as he thinks within himself, so he is." We become what we think. And what we think, we usually say.

You cannot receive what you don't believe. As we partnered with the Holy Spirit, we received His truth concerning health, allowed our minds to be renewed by the power of the Word, and began to think differently. We began to realize that the true value of God's Word is found in the believer, not in the Book. God's Word was never designed to just be words in a book; it was designed to be implanted in a believer. We must get it inside of us so that we can become its fulfillment.

As we got God's Word inside of us, we began to think differently. As we thought differently, we began to speak differently. This process was not easy. We still have to be guarded about what we say in order to speak only the truth. The stronghold of the enemy's lies gets so entrenched that sometimes we are not even aware of the lies we are confessing. For example, we catch ourselves saying, "I have a sweet tooth." Oops. As we think and believe, so we speak.

Is a sweet tooth something you believe you have, or do you confess that you no longer have a sweet tooth? I encourage you to memorize this truth about your words:

> Death and life are in the power of the tongue, and those who love it will eat its fruit.
>
> —PROVERBS 18:21

I do not know if we realize how powerfully creative the tongue is. According to God's Word, it is a driving force that brings forth life or death. As long as we spoke desire for the foods that were unhealthy, they had a hold on us. Our words created an open door for the flesh to be satisfied. By yielding to the Holy Spirit, we received truth that allowed us to change our confession to desire things that were good for our bodies, nourishing our health. We embraced these promises and spoke them creatively.

> A man will be satisfied with good by the fruit of his words.
>
> —PROVERBS 12:14

> The tongue of the wise brings healing.
>
> —PROVERBS 12:18

As we began to speak our desire for the good foods that we needed, we began to buy them and incorporate them into our diet. As we changed our diet, we began to see the fruit of our words manifested in our health. Our tongues brought healing to our bodies. What we thought, we believed. What we believed, we spoke. What we spoke, we received. That is what the Word of God can do.

Who Has Dominion?

In the beginning, when God gave man to rule over all creation, he was to cultivate the garden and keep it. The garden provided food for man to nourish him in health and allow him to reign in life and to have dominion over all the earth. When we are not in right standing with God, we lose our right to rule, our dominion. Things begin to get out of hand when man begins to rule without God.

The root of my problem was that food had dominion over me; I did not have dominion over food. For example, I loved to go into a bakery. But in the beginning, in the Garden of Eden, there were no bakeries. There were only plants that were good for food to nourish health. So many people declare they are allergic to "plants," almost any kind of vegetable or fruit. That is only true when they are living apart from redemption; we have dominion over all nutritional foods when we receive redemption.

As I began to walk in dominion over food, cultivating a nutritional diet and exercise plan, my body began to respond positively. It was as though my body was thanking me for feeding it good things. At first there was a little trauma with my flesh. My carnal nature screamed out its cravings for the bad stuff. But, as with any other kind of addiction, when the bad stuff was no longer in my body, the craving was gone.

As I continued giving my body the nutrients it needed for health, all of those life-threatening things that were wrong with my body began to disappear. No more obesity, no more heart disease, and no more blood pressure and cholesterol problems. God made our bodies to run on good nutrition. When I put the bad stuff in, I got a bad result. When I put the good stuff in, I got a good result. It is just that simple. Taking dominion over food was a tough process, but it has been life giving and satisfying to my entire being.

A God of Restoration

Sometimes we get so far out of shape or so sick we think God cannot restore us. The truth is that with God, all things are possible. When things get really bad, we can even begin to believe that maybe it is not

God's will to heal us. We may know His name is Jehovah Rapha, the God who heals, but because of our condition, we begin to doubt. It is as though we believe God is trying to decide whether to heal us or not. We must know it is always God's will to fulfill His will in us. That is why it is His will to heal us. His Word comes to us with fulfillment in it. Through Christ we have been made complete; Jesus is our restoration. I encourage you to receive His Word that promises to restore us. Throughout the Scriptures we read promises like this one:

> "For I will restore you to health and I will heal you of your wounds," declares the LORD.
>
> —JEREMIAH 30:17

Jesus is the fulfillment of this prophecy given hundreds of years before by the prophet Jeremiah. I found that when I applied the will of God to me, it brought restoration. I realized that God has already done all that He needs to do through Jesus. Now it is my responsibility to believe it, speak it, receive it, and walk in it. I realized that the promises of God are answered according to my faith. I had to believe that I received them:

> Therefore I say to you, all things for which you pray and ask, believe that you have received them, and they will be granted you.
>
> —MARK 11:24

In one sense, God did not have to *believe* anything; He wrote the Book. God is the Creator; we are the believers. When we believe, He creates. God is the beginning and the end. I realized that the responsibility for answered prayer was mine, not God's. This understanding created a major shift in my thinking. I am the one who has to believe that I receive at the time I pray and ask.

I used to believe only when I saw something. My attitude was that seeing is believing. In the kingdom of God, the opposite is true:

Believing is seeing. It does not take faith to believe what you can see. At sixty-four years of age, after God gave me a simple dream in which I became strong, I entered a life-changing process and became strong. That would have never happened if I walked by sight. Let me tell you, what I saw at the time was not pretty. I now realize when God gave me that prophetic dream that has been fulfilled, I had a Joel 2:28 experience:

> It will come about after this that I will pour out My Spirit on all mankind; and your sons and daughters will prophesy, your old men will dream dreams, your young men will see visions.

What I saw in the dream did not fit what I saw in my circumstances. I had to believe that the dream was from God and that I would become strong. So often, when God shows us something, we do not do anything about it because of unbelief. We do not believe because it does not fit our current circumstances. My dream certainly did not fit my current circumstances. The problem was that my current circumstances were outside the will of God. To get them inside the will of God, I had to *become* His will.

As I allowed the Holy Spirit to lead me, I experienced transformation in my life: spirit, soul, and body. In that transformation I became the strong man I saw in the dream. As I exercised my faith, I began to experience the reality that the will of God that saved my spirit began to redeem my body. I learned in dramatic fashion that our God is a God of restoration. I experienced in my health the wonderful promise given through the prophet Joel:

> And I will restore to you the years that the locust hath eaten.... And ye shall eat in plenty, and be satisfied, and praise the name of the LORD your God, that hath dealt wondrously with you: and my people shall never be ashamed.
>
> —JOEL 2:25–26, KJV

What God is saying is that if we partner with Him, it is never too late. He will make up the years lost to bad health. When we get older, we have a tendency to believe the lie, "I am too old to get strong as I once was." We live in a world that wants us to believe we have to live in the status quo. We have rest homes and convalescent hospitals waiting for us in our old age. We are supposed to get old, weak, and then fade away. God's Word promises that what He gives us in our younger years, He will give us in our latter years. The only thing that makes getting older equal getting weaker is our conduct. Living under the curse makes getting older mean getting weaker; living in redemption makes getting older simply mean getting wiser.

And our association brings assimilation. If we associate with the world's order, it will assimilate us into its beliefs. If we associate with God's order, it will transform us into believing and fulfilling His will. We can truly live long and strong when we take responsibility for proper stewardship. As God sustains us in our early years, He will sustain us in our latter years. His Word promises:

> Even to your old age I will be the same, and even to your graying years I will bear you! I have done it, and I will carry you; and I will bear you and I will deliver you.
> —ISAIAH 46:4

Now there is a promise to take to the bank of heaven. This tells us that even when we get older, God will be the power to sustain us. He will carry us as we acknowledge Him in our lives. He will deliver us from what the locust has stolen. How will He do this? By the power of His Spirit dwelling in us to quicken our mortal bodies with His resurrection power.

Light Is Power

As I partnered with the Holy Spirit to pursue my health, I began to think according to heaven's perspective instead of earth's. With the earthly perspective, I could only look up to heaven with a "Rapture mind-set," waiting for the Second Coming to let me escape the troubles of this earth. With my new heavenly perspective, I began to have a kingdom mind-set, expecting to see His kingdom come on earth.

I discovered that a religious spirit was causing me to live beneath my privileges as a son of God. I continually pictured myself at the cross of Jesus, which made me feel I was still bearing the sickness He had already borne for me. The Holy Spirit shone His light on that religious posture, and I discovered that the cross was only the entrance to my life in Christ; He wanted me to move beyond it into the fullness of His provision for abundant life (John 10:10). With that new understanding, I began to live in the life-giving power of Jesus.

As long as I stayed bowed before the cross in my thinking, I needed to explain why I was sick and unhealthy. But when I received faith to receive His resurrection power beyond the cross, I could explain why I was healed and healthy. I could move from an awareness of my sick condition to my position of health in Christ:

> Therefore if you have been raised up with Christ, keep seeking the things above, where Christ is, seated at the right hand of God. Set your mind on the things above, not on the things that are on earth.
>
> —Colossians 3:1–2

I truly began to realize the power of the light of God in my life to make me healthy and sustain my health when I took my rightful position in Christ. I understood that it is the enemy's goal to attack us with his fiery darts, his lies, in the realm of our spirit, our mind, and our body. But God's Word has made provision for our defense against him. The apostle Paul exhorts believers to make use of this divine defense:

> Finally, be strong in the Lord and in the strength of *His might*. Put on the full armor of God, so that you will be able to stand firm against the schemes of the devil.... in addition to all, taking up the shield of faith with which you will be able to extinguish *all* the flaming arrows of the evil one.
> —EPHESIANS 6:10–11, 16, EMPHASIS ADDED

We have been given divine protection in the armor of God. Note that it is not *our* armor that protects us; it is God's armor given to us that protects us. The apostle Paul refers to putting on the "armor of light" (Rom. 13:12). And the Scriptures teach that "God is Light" (1 John 1:5). As we learn to put on the armor of God, He makes us the light of the world (Matt. 5:14). Not only is that armor of light a defense for us, but it also helps us to show forth the life of Christ to others.

We know that light dispels darkness, and the Scriptures teach us to "walk as children of Light" (Eph. 5:8). When we have the light of God dwelling in us, we can lift the shield of faith to extinguish all the flaming missiles of the enemy. The reason we are not experiencing victory in our lives is because God's light is not shining brightly within our hearts and minds. Our light has been turned down, as though we have a dimmer switch that allows light to dissipate until we think we need it. Because darkness cannot coexist with light, our goal should be to become fully illumined with the light of God. Is that even possible? Jesus says it is:

> The eye is the lamp of your body; when your eye is clear, your whole body also is full of light.... If therefore your whole body is full of light, with no dark part in it, it will be *wholly illumined*, as when the lamp illumines you with its rays.
> —LUKE 11:34, 36, EMPHASIS ADDED

Jesus said that to be filled with light, your eye must be *clear*, which means "single, whole, sound."[15] Your whole body is full of light when your eyes see only what God sees. For that to happen, your mind must be renewed through revelation of His Word. Jesus taught us to allow our whole body to be filled with light. The words *wholly illumined* indicate that your body is composed of light.[16] In that illuminated condition, when your body is complete throughout, no darkness can exist.

This divine illumination represents a state of health for the physical body as well as the mind and spirit. It is our rightful position in Christ as we walk in His resurrection power. It is truly a spiritual reality that our whole being—spirit, mind, and body—is to be occupied by God Himself, who is light.

Walking in divine revelation

As the Holy Spirit began to teach me these truths, I recognized that some of the scriptures He showed me I had read before and thought they meant something different. When I used to read the Word with my fallen, "religious" mind-set, it did not bring life to me. But when the Holy Spirit brought the Word to me with a redeemed understanding, it came with life-changing power. Only the divine revelation of God's truth will give us breakthrough and set us free.

You cannot have breakthrough into abundant life unless you have a breakout. You must break out of old mind-sets that are not based in truth. You need to understand, for example, that it is not God's goal in redemption to simply get us to heaven; He is trying to get heaven into us. That is why He taught us to pray, "Thy kingdom come. Thy will be done in earth, as it is in heaven" (Matt. 6:10, KJV). At the Second Coming, Jesus is returning for a victorious church, not a failing one. For that to happen, it is obvious that as believers, we need more revelation of His Word. New revelation does not come by rehearsing what we knew yesterday. Setting our minds on things above will give us a heavenly perspective and fill us with His divine light.

Although your old self is corrupt, when your mind is renewed through redemption, it focuses on the life of the Spirit, which brings light to the flesh. The apostle Paul admonished believers to lay aside the old self that is corrupted and to "be renewed in the spirit of your mind" (Eph. 4:23).

What you see will determine who you are in the earth. As the head of His body in the earth, Jesus's eyes are to become your eyes. When you realize that you have been raised with Christ and seated in heavenly places with Him (Col. 3:1), your spiritual eyes will begin to see what He sees, your mind will be set on things above, and your body will be filled with His light. The condition of your body will be determined by the clarity of your spiritual sight. When you see what Jesus sees, you will see with the eyes of redemption, wholeness, and health.

How we see ourselves will also determine how the enemy sees us. The enemy always looks for an open door to our minds and heart to gain access with His lies. When we live in darkness, the enemy has power to harm us. Isaiah understood this divine principle:

> Woe to those…who substitute darkness for light and light for darkness.
>
> —ISAIAH 5:20

As a born-again Christian, darkness can only exist in your life when you choose to embrace it. God does not dwell in darkness; He is light. Darkness cannot exist in the light because light dispels it. The war between light and darkness is *our* struggle, not God's:

> For our struggle is not against flesh and blood, but against the rulers, against the powers, against the world forces of this darkness, against the spiritual forces of wickedness in the heavenly places.
>
> —EPHESIANS 6:12

God is not worried about the devil; he is a defeated foe because of Christ's death and resurrection. We only need to worry about the devil when our "dimmer switch" is turned down—when we are not focused on the light of God. When God, who is light, shows up, darkness cannot exist. It is our responsibility to keep our eye single, to focus only on the light of God.

In the daytime when you are in a dark building and you turn the light on, do you run outside to see where the darkness went? You understand that light dispelled the darkness. Darkness only affects us if we choose to embrace it. The enemy shows us his power of darkness in sickness or some other negative condition for the sole purpose of getting us to embrace it with our belief system.

If the light of God within us is greater than the enemy's darkness, that darkness will be swallowed up, completely dispelled by divine light. With the full armor of God in place, we are able to resist the devil's lies. We cannot resist him in our strength, but we can resist him in the strength of God that He provides for us. We can be victorious in our struggle against the forces of darkness as we allow the Holy Spirit to occupy our lives fully.

In other words, when the enemy tries to tell you his lies, he is attempting to cover the truth, God's light, with darkness. Jesus called the devil the father of lies (John 8:44). His lies will try to cover up truth, but truth has evidence the lie does not. Part of the problem keeping the church from living in victory is that we are acknowledging the work of the enemy too much. We will not have to acknowledge His lies of darkness if we are full of light. God warns us about living in darkness:

> Then watch out that the light in you may not be darkness.
>
> —LUKE 11:35

How can *light* be darkness? The Greek word translated "light" in Luke 11:35 refers to artificial light emitted by a lamp or torch.[17] If you allow a mixture of light and darkness to dim the light of God within, it will constantly keep you from reaching the fullness of abundant life, or wholeness, in God. When you look at what the enemy does and believe he has the power to make you sick, you choose not to believe God, who has greater power to make you well.

As a new creation, you are to be continually filled with the light of God. When your eye is clear, your whole body will be full of light. And in that heavenly light, any darkness emanating from the enemy will be extinguished. This is the goal for which we must strive: a fully illumined body, a body of health where sickness (darkness) cannot exist. It is obtainable in Christ; with God all things are possible.

The "Occupied Man"

Revelation of what I call the "occupied man" set me free from my struggles to overcome powers of darkness that robbed me of Christ's abundant life. I understand there are different connotations to the word *occupy*. I am referring to being fully occupied by the Holy Spirit as someone who is wholly filled with Him, in the same way a container that cannot hold one more drop of water would be "fully occupied." In my Christian life, while the Holy Spirit was available to me, I did not fully embrace Him or allow Him complete access to every area of my life. I was constantly trying to better myself. I felt I was not good enough. I seemed to be pursuing a different self-help program every month.

I was born again, and I had God in my life. Then I heard the Holy Spirit say, "You have to let Me change your mind. You are not to see yourself as a man who has God; it is God who has a man." I began to understand that a part-time God can only give us a part-time result. Of course, it was not God who had been part-time; it was my availability to God that had been part-time. My will was not totally given to Him so that He could fully occupy me and have complete control of my life.

I listened intently as He continued, "You are created in the image of God, and through redemption, you have become the possession of God: God has you. You are to become a man occupied—filled up with—the Spirit of God. Recognize that it is no longer you who lives, but Christ is living in you by His Spirit (Gal. 2:20). Embracing this truth will set you free. Now all things will be possible for you because it will not be you doing them, but God doing them through you."

As I meditated on this wonderful revelation, I figured that if it is not I who lives, then somebody has to die. And I was sure that was not going to be God. I also realized that you only need resurrection power when you are dead. When I was focused on my natural life and myself, there was no power. When I set my mind on God's life within me, power was never a problem. The Holy Spirit opened my understanding to understand that old things are passed away. He said to me, "Those were the things *you* had. All things have become new; those are the things *I* have." When I realized that I did not have anything to add to God's power, a huge burden came off my back.

I began to understand what the Word means when Christ said to the apostle Paul, "[My] power is perfected in weakness" (2 Cor. 12:9). That word prompted Paul to declare that he would rather boast about his weakness so that the power of Christ would make Him strong (v. 10). It was God's power, not Paul's, that worked signs and wonders and miracles through him. The spiritual reality is that, as a born-again believer, you are a God-occupied man or woman. God simply wants your will to align with His will. When this happens, you become the fulfillment of His will in the earth.

True freedom came to me when I realized that through redemption, I now have His life in me. Too often, even as Christians, we want *our* life and *our* will fulfilled. I think the reason so many Christians get so tired is because they are fighting to maintain this separation between their will and God's. If you are His body, there can be no separation. Jesus promised that if you would abide in Him, He would abide in you and that you could "ask whatever you wish, and it will be done for you" (John 15:7). What is it that will be done for you? His will shall be done for you, in you, and through you in the earth.

God created you as a new creation so that you could show forth His glory on the earth. God, the Creator in heaven, lives inside of you to make you creative on earth. God wants to have total possession of you so that you can glorify Him in the earth. When you reach that goal, you will be free from your limited ability and will release His supernatural ability in you. When you are totally occupied by Christ, you will be totally God supplied. Then it is not only who you are in Christ; it becomes who Christ is in you!

When you are fully occupied by the Spirit, it is not you *and* God; it is God *in* you. He did not come to save your life; He came to give you His divine life. There is no real life apart from God. This is not about deifying your flesh; it is about the Deity fully occupying the flesh, making you complete in Him. As we prepare to consider the power of receiving impartation of truth in the next chapter, let's review this wonderful truth of being complete in Christ:

> For in Him all the fullness of Deity dwells in bodily form, and in Him you have been made complete, and He is the head over all rule and authority.
>
> —COLOSSIANS 2:9–10

The key to living the abundant life in Christ is to be fully occupied with God so that He is glorified in your body, mind, and spirit. This "occupied" man or woman will reflect the light of God in wholeness and health.

Chapter 4

TRUTH THAT OVERCOMES FACTS

An impartation of truth will not
"return void" (Isa. 55:11, NKJV).

There is a wonderful promise in the book of Isaiah that applies to our lives as believers who are pursuing God through revelation of His Word:

> For as the rain and the snow come down from heaven, and do not return there without watering the earth and making it bear and sprout, and furnishing seed to the sower and bread to the eater; so will My word be which goes forth from My mouth; it will not return to Me empty [void], without accomplishing what I desire, and without succeeding in the matter for which I sent it.
> —Isaiah 55:10–11

As I began to discover the truth of healing Jesus brought to us, I realized that it was God's will that I walk totally free from sickness and live in health. His redemption gave me the right to no longer live under the curse of sin and sickness. But to truly be set free from that curse, I realized I needed a fresh revelation of truth.

When I read the Word of God, I thought it was God's responsibility to fulfill His Word in my life. My only responsibility was to wait for God to do His will. So in situations where it appeared God didn't do anything, I got frustrated. I would say to Him, "Well, You said it; why aren't You doing it?" Then God said to me, "I am not the doer; I am the Creator. When you do, I create." Suddenly I realized that my responsibility was more than to just wait for God to do His will.

He reminded me of Mark 11:24: "All things for which you pray and ask, believe that you have received them, and they will be granted you." He wanted me to know His Word is a creative power, but its creativity will be released as it works through the faith of a believer. Praying, asking, believing—these were my responsibility to release the will of God in my life. God doesn't need faith; I do. As we activate our faith, it becomes the vehicle that brings His will into our life. Our faith is in the Word, which is called seed. When we plant the seed of truth in our hearts, God can bring forth His will, which is our total redemption.

The Holy Spirit revealed to me that I was living my life in "natural reality" rather than His kingdom reality. In observing natural reality, I was going by facts that I could see. The problem with this mentality is that in the world, *facts* are called truth. I was walking by sight and believing that facts of natural reality were true. I needed to understand that God's Word is truth and that God's truth is greater than any natural fact. Jesus prayed that God would sanctify His disciples in the truth: "Thy word is truth" (John 17:17, KJV). His truth is His creative power to transform our "facts" into redemptive reality.

When the devil tells you that you are *sick*, which looks like fact, you need to believe the greater truth of God that you are *healed*. As you bring the kingdom of God to earth through faith, you move in redemptive truth. What is unredeemed is factual; what is redeemed is kingdom truth. Kingdom truth brings redemptive order into your life, which subdues natural facts to the will of God. When the Creator wrote the Book, His will revealed in that Book was creative. The truth of God is alive; it is not a dead letter: "For the word of God is living and active and sharper than any two-edged sword..." (Heb. 4:12).

The truth of God comes with fulfillment resident within it. That is why He says His Word will not return void (empty), without accomplishing what He desires (Isa. 55:11). Truth has evidence in it; the lie of the enemy is based on no real evidence. Kingdom truth will always trump natural facts. The responsibility for establishing God's truth in the earth is ours. Jesus said, "You will know the truth, and the truth will make you free" (John 8:32). God does not need to *know* the truth; He is the Truth; He wrote the Book. Jesus declared, "I am the way, and the truth, and the life" (John 14:6). We are the ones who need to know the truth. When we know Him and walk according to God's will, He who personifies truth will set us free; the life of Christ makes the will of God creative. When we understand this principle, we can move into God's kingdom reality.

I had to ask myself, "What is more real, the created or the Creator who created it?" Only when I understood that the Creator is more real than the "created" natural facts I see could I begin to move in the truth of God that would deliver me from those natural facts. Without this revelation, I could not believe it was possible to walk in true health. I discovered that my life does not determine my lifestyle. It is my lifestyle that determines my life. When my lifestyle lines up with the life of Christ within me, then my life begins to change.

I had to change my lifestyle by embracing the truth that with God *all* things, even health, are possible. My deliverance was not determined by where I was in natural circumstances but by who I was in Christ. I am a man occupied by God; His Spirit lives in me. I can do all things by Him, and no weapon formed against me can prosper. I began to walk according to the living will of God that was being established in me through faith in His Word.

The Seed

The Word of God is called seed (Luke 8:11) because, like natural seed that sprouts when placed in the earth, the Word becomes living and active when we plant it in our heart by faith. Jesus was the first seed that God planted in the earth, and we are His offspring, born again by the seed of the Word: "For you have been born again not of seed which is perishable but imperishable, that is, through the living and enduring word of God" (1 Pet. 1:23).

We are born again by the Word of God that cannot perish; it is eternal life to us. It is life that continues to grow and produce harvest. It is creative in us and will not fail us as long as we apply our faith to it: "But it is easier for heaven and earth to pass away than for one stroke of a letter of the Law to fail" (Luke 16:17). Heaven and earth will pass away before any part of the seed of God's Word could fail.

The seed carries the increase within itself. God does not have to decide to increase it. He backs it up as we become colaborers with Him: "God also testifying with them, both by signs and wonders and by various miracles and by gifts of the Holy Spirit according to His own will" (Heb. 2:4). The phrase "also testifying with them" means "to testify further jointly or to unite in adding evidence."[1] The Spirit of God unites His will with us like seed sprouting in a believer in order for fruit to be produced. Jesus described the harvest of the seed of His Word planted in good soil:

> But the seed in the good soil, these are the ones who have heard the word in an honest and good heart, and hold it fast, and bear fruit with perseverance.
>
> —LUKE 8:15

The Word of God has evidence in it because it is "truth seed" waiting to produce fruit when it is planted in a believer's heart of faith. Here again, the increase is inherent in the seed. The Word, which is seed, becomes creative when it is planted in us. God does not have to decide to make it creative; He has already done that. His will is already fulfilled by Him and is now waiting to be fulfilled in us.

My Peach Seed

When I was a young man living in the country, peaches were my favorite fruit. I loved peaches. One day I was in the kitchen eating a big juicy peach, leaning over the sink because it was dripping. I remember thinking, "I am going to eat this peach, then go outside and plant the seed so that I could grow a peach tree and have all the peaches I want." My mom came into the kitchen and asked me, "Why do you seem to be in such a hurry to eat that peach?" I told her that I was going out right away and plant the seed. She said, "No, you must put the seed in the window sill and let it dry out first." I did not understand why I needed to do that, but my mom said so, so I did it.

A few weeks later I went into the kitchen to get a cold drink of water on a hot day and noticed the peach seed I had left on the sill. Mom said, "It is time to plant the seed." So I took that peach seed out to the field, dug a round trench for water, and planted the seed in the middle of it. Living in the country, I knew about seedtime and harvest; I did not plant the seed then come out the next day thinking I would see it sprouting. I knew that if I continued to water it, in due time, the seed would grow. I knew that resident in the life in that seed was a peach tree waiting to spring forth. When God created the peach seed, He put the DNA of a peach tree in it.

The seed would become creative when I planted it in the right environment. I could have carried that seed around with me as long as I wanted and could have asked God, "Why haven't You given me my peach harvest?" As long as I have that seed in my pocket, I have the promise of the harvest. But I cannot receive the harvest unless I act upon the seed. It is not God's responsibility to plant the seed; it is mine. He created it with life in it; I must plant it to reap the benefits of that life.

In that same way, for the harvest of personal redemption, healing, or souls to come to the earth, I have to be a doer of the Word, not just a hearer (James 1:23). When I partner with God, who supplies seed for the sower, I plant; He brings the increase (2 Cor. 9:10–11). Too often I see Christians who are waiting for God to bring a desired harvest when they have not planted the seed.

I have seen others who plant the seed one day and the next day dig it up to see if it is growing. Faith requires us to be patient and leave the seed in the ground until it receives the early and late rains (James 5:7). It is what we do with what we do not see that determines what we do see. Faith requires us to believe the increase is coming. If I did not believe the increase was in the seed, I would not have planted it. Jesus said the Word planted in the good heart would hold it fast and "bear fruit with perseverance" (Luke 8:15). Like a good farmer, we have to water it, pull the weeds, and wait patiently, believing we are going to receive the harvest from the Word planted in us. The whole reason God gives us seed is to bless us with His divine benefits. The psalmist declared, "Blessed be the Lord, who daily loadeth us with benefits, even the God of our salvation" (Ps. 68:19, KJV).

The Scriptures teach that God is a rewarder of those who believe Him and diligently seek Him (Heb. 11:6). He wants His will fulfilled in us because of His love for us. I am sad when I see Christians who do not plant and water the seed of God's Word and then blame God because they do not receive a harvest. I once did the same thing. We sometimes blame God for not healing us though we believe He is a healer. Faith for healing is our responsibility to appropriate His promise to heal. If we put that responsibility on God, we do not exercise faith as He has commanded us to do.

Faith-Driven Seed

When I first picked up that peach seed, I became responsible for the harvest it contained. If I wanted a harvest of peaches, I had to understand how to bring it forth by faith. I had to walk in faith, believing in

God's law of sowing and reaping. I had to plant the seed, then water it without seeing anything but wet dirt, which meant walking in the unseen realm for a season. My faith caused me to believe in what I could not see. It was my faith in the life resident in that peach seed that established my belief. When I possessed the seed, I knew I had the harvest in my future. It was my faith in the seed that established my future.

Applying the truth of this analogy to my faith for healing (my harvest) caused me to partner with the Holy Spirit to become healthy. I had to understand the part I was going to play and the part God was going to play. I first needed seed: the truth of God's Word. Was it God's will that I walk in health? I had assurance from His Word that it was His will that I be whole, complete in Christ. I declared my faith in the seed without seeing the reality: "Now faith is the assurance of things hoped for, the conviction of things not seen" (Heb. 11:1).

You cannot have a harvest without faith. All the seed in the world would not help the farmer if he did not have the faith that it would produce a harvest. The Word of God produces faith so that you can reap a harvest: "So faith comes from hearing, and hearing by the word of Christ" (Rom. 10:17). It is the seed that produces faith; it is our faith that brings the harvest. This is kingdom partnership with God. He supplies the seed; when we receive that seed, it produces faith; our faith brings the harvest. Faith is the requirement for us to receive the harvest; it is also the requirement to please God:

> And without faith it is impossible to please Him, for he who comes to God must believe that He is and that He is a rewarder of those who seek Him.
>
> —HEBREWS 11:6

It is impossible to please God without faith. Without faith you cannot fulfill His will. Faith is simply trusting that God will do what

He says. God's Word says it is easier for heaven and earth to pass away than for His Word to fail. When I held that peach seed in my hand, my faith in the life of that seed was the assurance of the tree that I hoped for. I did not have to see the tree to believe it was coming; that seed had the evidence in it.

The power of hope

I remember making statements in the past like, "Well, I would have more faith, but I do not want to get my hopes too high." I did not realize that in Hebrews 11:1, the Greek word for *hope* means "trust."[2] So, what I was actually saying was, "I do not want to *trust* God too much." I began to understand that the only reason I did not want to get my hopes too high was because I was trying to measure a future hope by a past failure. And the reason I had the past failure was because I was not walking in faith anyway. I was trying to determine my future by evaluating my past, which is a recipe for failure.

The enemy took advantage of my faulty thinking process and would cause a past failure to appear to be a present reality in my life. It does not require faith to believe in our past. The important thing about our past is that it is past, over, finished. We now have a future that can set us into the will of God by faith. Hope relates only to the future, something promised and yet to come.

When I had the dream in which I saw myself become strong, I had to begin to trust God for that to happen. My past said that at sixty-four years of age this could not happen. But my future was set before me by the faith produced in me with that God-given dream. I declared in faith the will of God He revealed to me: "With men this is impossible; but with God all things are possible" (Matt. 19:26, KJV). My faith allowed me to see what God saw. The goal of my faith was that future reality of living in health. My hope was to be strong, no longer sick. The evidence of that, in the beginning, was not seen, but my faith in God's promise was the substance of strength.

As I walked out my faith, I became stronger each day. My faith then created a future that no longer reflected past failure. Our faith will always move the will of God into its creative power so that we receive the promise. Faith is not subject to past failures. Actually, if you think about it, our faith assigns the Holy Spirit to the fulfillment of the will of God for our future.

It was this revelation of the power of hope that began to change my life. God wants His will done on earth as it is in heaven (Matt. 6:10). When we become new creatures in Christ, He occupies us with His Spirit. The Spirit of God dwelling in us provides the power within to cause the will of God to become creative in our lives. Our faith becomes the vehicle for the unseen things of God to be seen on the earth. This is simply the way God works in us. When my will and His will agree, faith is activated so that the Holy Spirit can release His power to cause the seed (His Word) to produce a harvest.

I know that some people have difficulty believing we can partner with a holy God. It would not be possible if we were still living under the curse of sin. It is God Himself who cleansed us by the blood of Jesus and put His Spirit within us when we were born again. The Scriptures teach that God made Christ, who knew no sin, to be sin on our behalf, that we might become the righteousness of God in Christ (2 Cor. 5:21). In other words, we now are in right standing with God. And God tells us we can come boldly into His presence as members of His family:

> For through Him we both have our access in one Spirit to the Father. So then you are no longer strangers and aliens, but you are fellow citizens with the saints, and are of God's household.
> —EPHESIANS 2:18–19

We are not strangers to God, separated from Him. As fellow citizens together, we can be fully "occupied" by the Spirit of God, who gives us access to our heavenly Father. The purpose of redemption is so that God can have a relationship with His children. If we persist in our fallen nature mind-set, we will we not embrace this wonderful reality. Remember, the condition we are in is determined by the position we take before God. Embracing God's truth will determine our position and set us free from every destructive condition.

Problem of hope deferred

In order to allow faith to prevail in my life, I had to deal with my faulty concept of hope. The Holy Spirit had to show me the difference between the hope that brought success and the "hope so" that brought failure. In the Old Testament, *hope* was a strong word that meant "to wait in expectancy."[3] We discussed that, in Hebrews 11:1, faith is the substance of things "hoped for." We see there that hope filled with the substance of God's will shall manifest in the lives of believers.

Unfortunately, the word *hope* has been distorted and diluted to mean something we don't dare to believe will happen. For example, when someone says that the drought will be over soon, we may respond, "I sure hope so." That is not hope; it is actually expressing doubt that it will happen. In that mind-set, our true hope is often delayed, which makes us heartsick:

> Hope deferred makes the heart sick, but desire fulfilled is a tree of life.
>
> —PROVERBS 13:12

When I walked by sight, focusing on my condition, my hope of healing seemed deferred or delayed, which made me heartsick. In my "hope-so" mind-set, I would hope I would be healed. I would hope I could walk in health. There was little trust in that kind of hope. I was living with a hope-so faith rather than a know-so faith. The danger with this mentality is that it cuts off faith rather than establishing it. This kind of hope was holding off my healing rather than establishing it. It made me receptive to the very sickness from which I wanted to be set free.

I had to exchange my "hope-so" mind-set for God's truth. Faith in God's truth must cause us to know we are healed so that we can confess those things that are not as though they are. It doesn't take faith to see sickness. It takes faith to believe God's Word that says, "I am healed," rather than believing what we see. What I realized was that when I hoped I was healed, what I *knew* was that I was not healed; that is what I believed. True hope establishes faith that takes our healing; "hope-so" unbelief delays our promise.

The farmer who knows the increase is in the seed plants it in faith that the harvest is coming. Just like the farmer, we exercise faith in the natural world all the time. For example, a mother may have a vision for dessert for her family, perhaps a chocolate cake with chocolate frosting. So she puts all of the ingredients (substance) for the cake on the kitchen counter. She needs flour, sugar, milk, and other ingredients. But she does not prepare all the ingredients but then looks up to heaven and says, "Oh, God, please give me a cake." She knows she has to mix them together, put "the substance" in the oven, and turn up the fire.

When Scripture says that faith is the *substance* of things hoped for, the substance is a reality greater than what it produces. It is a kingdom reality that faith, the substance of the promise, is more real than what it produces. In the example of the mom, which was more real—the substance or the cake? If you do not believe the substance is more real, try to "create" the cake without the substance.

We do not realize how much faith we exercise in common, everyday situations. If you invited me over to your house tomorrow night for dinner at 6:00 p.m., what would you be doing at 5:00 p.m. tomorrow? You would probably be preparing the meal and straightening up the house. At 5:30 p.m. you would not likely say to your spouse, "Let's go out to dinner tonight." And when the doorbell rings at 6:00 p.m., you probably would not wonder, "Who could that be?" You are exercising faith that because I accepted your invitation to dinner, I will show up. And you answer the door to greet me.

Why is it so easy to have faith for a guest to show up and so hard to have faith for God to show up? Sometimes I think the problem is that God is showing up as He promised at 6:00 p.m. and nobody is home. We need to trust God that He will show up according to His promise: He is a rewarder of those who seek Him (Heb. 11:6). True faith does not deny that you are sick or ignore your condition. Instead, it establishes that you are healed according to the promise. Faith is the substance that establishes a position of health, releasing God's creative power to overcome any condition of sickness:

> For whatever is born of God overcomes the world; and this is the victory that has overcome the world—our faith.
>
> —1 JOHN 5:4

The truth of God's Word declares that, as believers, we are born of God and can overcome the world. To walk in this victory, we must exercise our faith. The Greek word for *overcome* means "to conquer, to carry off the victory."[4] Our faith is the means to victory in establishing the will of God on the earth.

The "Sound" of His Will

In the Book of Genesis, the biblical account of creation declares that when God spoke, the sound of His voice was creative: "And God said, Let there be light: and there was light" (Gen. 1:3, KJV). When the Creator speaks, creation happens. And what He created in turn became creative. God blessed all of His creation, saying, "Be fruitful and multiply" (v. 22). Fish create fish, birds create birds, animals create animals, trees create trees, plants create plants, and people create people. The sound of the voice of the Creator produced life forms that are creative. When the Creator creates creation, creation becomes creative. You cannot be created in the image and likeness of God and not be creative. We are *not* God, but as born-again Christians we are the children of God (1 John 3:2).

In the beginning God walked with Adam and Eve in the garden: "And they heard the voice of the LORD God walking in the garden in the cool of the day" (Gen. 3:8, KJV). All creation was good. Creation was releasing a sound coming from a world at peace. Only after the Fall did that sound change. After mankind's disobedience, there entered the sound that comes from fear, terror, anger, pain, and suffering. It was a frightening sound—the sound of poverty, sickness, and death. It was that sound from mankind that caused division between father and mother and son and daughter; it was the sound of a lost dominion. This sound was no longer creative in the positive sense; though it continued to multiply in the earth, the sound of creation became destructive.

Earlier I mentioned the power of the tongue, the sound we make, which Scripture says can bring life or death (Prov. 18:21). Whether for good or evil, our tongue is still a creative force. In the New Testament, the apostle James wrote that the tongue is a fire, a world of iniquity that is set on fire by hell (James 3:6). He said that we use our tongues to bless God and curse men; then he warned, "My brethren, these things ought not to be this way" (v. 10).

James wrote that even though the tongue is a small part of the body, "... it boasts of great things. See how great a forest is set aflame by such a small fire!" (v. 5). It is important for a believer to understand that the sound we release with our tongues is truly creative. It can build up, or it can tear down. When our tongue is speaking the truth of God, it will release creative life. Jesus, through redemption, restored to us the ability to speak life. The Creator creates the word of His will, which is living and active, in the believer as seed that will produce a harvest.

According to the Scriptures, hearing the Word of God produces faith in our hearts. We need to speak faith so that it is heard on the earth. Faith requires us to confess those things that are not as though they were (Heb. 11:1). We must understand that the sound we release will either create the will of God or the will of the enemy. It will produce creative life or destructive death. The sound we release will reflect what we believe in our hearts. Only when we are led by the Holy Spirit can we release the creative sound of His will. Then we reap the harvest of good seed sown in faith:

> For it is God who is at work in you, both to will and to work for His good pleasure.
>
> —PHILIPPIANS 2:13

As I used my tongue to speak the will of God over my health, the "sound" of God's will came into my natural body and created the supernatural will of God. I had courage and strength to steward my body toward health and make lifestyle changes that matched my confession. Things don't happen just because I say them; they do happen when I agree with God's will and declare what He says. Faith requires us to say something. If the Word does not have a voice, it cannot be heard in the earth.

Had I spoken the will of the enemy, my confession would have continued to create my sick condition. I would have confessed all the reasons why I could not become healthy and strong. I would have continued my poor lifestyle choices without hope of making positive changes. That confession would have come from an unrenewed mind living under the curse of sin.

Listen to what you say.

It is very important for you to listen to what you say. Your confession always comes from your established belief system. And it works with God or the enemy to create either life or death. Your success is not determined by the people around you but by the God who is in you to do His good pleasure.

I could believe I was going to become strong because I had faith that it was God's will for me. My faith required me to speak what I did not yet see but knew was coming. In other words, I planted the seed and spoke to the harvest of health I wanted to see. When the sound we release is God driven, it will produce a demonstration of creative power. The apostle confirms this principle:

> And my message and my preaching were not in persuasive words of wisdom, but in demonstration of the Spirit and of power, so that your faith should not rest on the wisdom of men, but on the power of God. Yet we do speak wisdom among those who are mature; a wisdom, however, not of this age nor of the rulers of this age, who are passing away; but we speak God's wisdom in a mystery, the hidden wisdom which God predestined before the ages to our glory; the wisdom which none of the rulers of this age has understood.
>
> —1 Corinthians 2:4–8

This is an amazing scripture. The apostle Paul's faith, established in the Word of God, when spoken forth carried with it a demonstration of the Spirit and of power. That *demonstration* meant there was "proof, a manifestation, a showing forth of God's power."[5] It tells us that when our faith is established by the Word of God, and we speak it, there will be a demonstration of the Spirit and of power. That demonstration is the creative fulfillment of God's will.

Our faith is the substance of something we hope for, and that substance is waiting to take shape. When we speak our faith, our voice becomes the sound of God's will in the natural realm. Supernatural power rushes to be a demonstration of the creative power to manifest "what is not." That is when creation takes place and God's will is done on the earth as it is in heaven. When Jesus spoke, "Be healed," His words caused a demonstration of Spirit and power in the earth. What had not existed was created, and sickness existed no longer.

The will of God is to be spoken and heard on the earth. When the Word of God is heard, faith is created; the Word of God is the voice of God to our faith. We hear it so that we can speak it. We speak so that we can create the will of God in our situation. I am encouraged that all over the earth today the sound of faith is being released and people are being changed. In our healing rooms we see people who have been deeply hurt by words, lives that carry pain caused by words that tear down and destroy. And when God's Word is spoken to them, they receive healing for their deep wounds.

Truly, as believers, we must understand that what we speak can be creative or destructive. If we are to walk in health, we have to speak words of faith for health. A life of health is in the power of the tongue. Too often I hear people who are unhealthy make fun of those who are trying to walk in health. This has a tendency to justify their own condition rather than help them change their position.

The enemy sets up strongholds in our unrenewed minds that must be broken by speaking the truth of God. As I discussed, speaking alone will not "bake the cake." But speaking words of faith regarding your health position will motivate and empower you to supernatural wisdom and power for the fulfillment of God's will. We use words all day long, but do they contain power?

I discovered that to be successful on this journey of faith for health, my words had to speak the health I desired. Before I began my journey, my words lined up with what made me unhealthy. I spoke *good* words about *bad* food choices. For example, I talked about how delicious fried foods were and how much I loved chocolate. I even had a chocolate drawer in the office that I always kept well supplied. What I spoke regarding unhealthy foods resulted in unhealthy actions. Jesus taught us:

For by your words you will be justified, and by your words you
will be condemned.

—MATTHEW 12:37

Walking in health in this world is not easy; you have to choose it,
but the reward for the effort is life. I had to begin to speak in faith
what I believed about my pursuit of health. My words had to establish
the will of God in my life. I had to see myself healthy and strong. My
age was not going to determine my health; my God was. I began to
speak the promise of the Word to create my healing: "The tongue of
the wise brings healing" (Prov. 12:18).

I spoke to my wife and I spoke to my staff that I was going to become
strong. I could speak this because I believed it. The sound of my voice
heard by those around me began to fill them with expectation for my
success. As I planted that seed of faith in them, they began to water
the seed. They would encourage me by asking "How is your workout
going?" They would comment on how good I was looking. When you
are in your midsixties and someone says, "You are looking younger,"
it is like throwing a bone to a dog. The good results I was experiencing
became contagious. The "sound" around the office began to change. It
became a healthy sound, filled with expectation and encouragement—
the sound of life abundantly.

The Knower

For me to become strong, I had to know that I could arrive in that
place of strength. If we leave our house to go to the market, we have
to first see ourselves arriving there. If we do not know the destination
ahead of time, we cannot arrive. It is what we *know* that determines
where we go.

> You have an anointing from the Holy One, and you all *know*. I have not written to you because you do not know the truth, but because you do *know* it, and because no lie is of the truth.
> —1 JOHN 2:20–21, EMPHASIS ADDED

The Holy Spirit had to tap into my "knower" with His truth so that I could see myself strong when I was not. This is called vision. Vision requires us to see what is not yet there. I had to know something so that I could see something. It all starts with knowing truth. When I did not know God's will, I could not become strong in spirit, mind, *and* body, so I was perishing in body.

> Therefore My people go into exile for their lack of knowledge; and their honorable men are famished, and their multitude is parched with thirst.
> —ISAIAH 5:13

Living in exile, a place of captivity, is the result of living with a lack of knowledge. When I did not know I could be healthy in body, I lived in captivity to sickness. When you have a heart attack, you know you are in captivity. I began to understand that as a leader in the body of Christ, I have a responsibility to bring health not only to the spirit and the mind but also to the *body* of the church. Too many of God's people are perishing because the body of Christ does not know how to become healthy by speaking the will of God in faith through the Spirit of God that dwells in them. The body of Christ will prosper when we speak our knowledge of truth:

> A wise man is strong, and a man of knowledge increases power. For by wise guidance you will wage war, and in abundance of counselors there is victory.
> —PROVERBS 24:5–6

Strength, power, and boldness are promised to the wise and those who have knowledge. You cannot experience boldness when you are weak and afflicted. Wisdom is the proper application of knowledge. It is not enough to have knowledge; we must apply knowledge with wisdom so that we increase in power. It is not enough to know how to become strong. We must receive wisdom from the Holy Spirit in order to apply what we know to our life. Guiding each other with wisdom will help us to wage war, to do battle against the destructive forces that diminish our strength and health. From a point of strength and power we can achieve victory against the destructive plans of the evil one. The strength and power of God in us will determine the outcome. When I figured out that we win this fight of faith, it changed the way I fought. A winner will overwhelmingly conquer.

The way we *know* in the kingdom of God is different from what we know in the natural world. In the kingdom you know by faith. In the natural you know by what you see. In the kingdom you must *know* something exists by faith without seeing it. Vision sees what is not yet seen in the natural and brings it to manifestation. It sees what is coming. Through vision the kingdom of God comes upon the earth. In other words, when you know and ask according to God's will, truth is activated to create the evidence of God's will manifested upon the earth. Only when you know something exists in the supernatural can you speak in faith to establish it in the natural realm. The power to demonstrate God's will flows through your "knower," which then places a demand on what is unseen to become seen:

> This is the confidence which we have before Him, that, if we ask anything according to His will, He hears us. And if we *know* that He hears us in whatever we ask, we *know* that we have the request which we have asked from Him.
>
> —1 JOHN 5:14–15, EMPHASIS ADDED

According to this amazing scripture, we must first ask according to His will. Secondly, when we do that, God hears us when we ask according to His will. Thirdly, when we *know* He hears us, we can expect to receive whatever we have asked for. It does not say you *might* get what you ask for or that God will decide whether or not to give it to you. It says that when you *know* He hears you, you can know you have what you have asked.

Asking according to His will is like planting seed and reaping a harvest. The reason you have it is because it is already God's will for you. The impartation of divine truth, God's will, is a word that will not return "empty"; it brings increase that fulfills His will. Again, the power to demonstrate God's will in your life flows through your "knower." It is your knowing that gives you the confidence to receive, by faith, what you ask for.

The measure of your *doing* the will of God is determined by the measure of your *knowing*. When you know the truth, faith locks into truth, and then truth becomes creative to establish God's will in your life. You create God's will with the substance of faith you receive from that realm of divine truth. How do you create? Not in your own strength, but by the power of the Spirit of God who dwells in you.

In this way the truth and power of heaven invade the earth. You cannot have an invasion until the troops show up. The kingdom of God cannot come to this earth unless we, as believers, show up. If the kingdom of God is within us, then we are the ones who have to allow it to manifest in the earth. Through knowing God's will and receiving it by faith, we become the fulfillment of God's will on the earth. God's will is fulfilled perfectly in heaven, but it is not yet fulfilled perfectly on the earth. He is working His will in us to reveal it in the earth and establish His kingdom through us.

The Opposition

This message of walking in stewardship of our body, the temple of God, and experiencing physical health is not welcomed without opposition. When the Holy Spirit brings new revelation to the church, it requires that we embrace change. I have noticed we do not like change. Personally, I understand how difficult it is to receive the truth of change because this is how I used to live. I attended church for twenty-five years and lived a religious life. I operated in a "form of godliness" but denied its power (2 Tim. 3:5) because I opposed the idea of change.

There was no supernatural power exhibited in my life; I thought sitting in the church pew was my destiny. Then I discovered that when Jesus said to "occupy till I come" (Luke 19:13, KJV), He was not talking about "occupying" a church pew. I was involved passively in a form of religion that was in opposition to any movement of God in the church. A religious spirit caused me to operate by sight and make sure that nothing changed. When you are in bondage to a religious spirit, you cannot process truth because religion establishes form, not power.

Revelation of truth is given so that we can step into it to fulfill it. Truth can only set us free as we move from being a *knower* to becoming a *doer*. When I began to share the truth I had learned regarding this health message, some people did not like it; they opposed it. The opposition would say, "That can't be God. We can't talk about health in the church."

Yet how can we say that God is not interested in a healthy church? One thing I know is that the devil does not want us healthy. How can we as believers receive life for our spirit, renew our minds with the truth, and let our body fall apart? One person said to me, "We don't need to tell people they are obese or that their body is unhealthy. They already know that. Telling them will just cause them to feel condemnation." What if we used that logic with those who are sick? They already know they are sick. Why address their condition? They may feel condemned. There can be no help for the needy unless we address, with compassion, their unhealthy condition. Jesus was always moved by compassion for the deliverance of captives.

The Scriptures declare that, no matter our condition as believers, there is "no condemnation for those who are in Christ Jesus" (Rom. 8:1). We are all in need of help to be redeemed from every vestige of bondage and sin. It is our responsibility as the body of Christ to reach out, in love, to everyone who is hurting. Knowing that it is God's will that we walk in health, we must encourage one another in this truth. It is not about where we are; it is about where we are going. God is not as concerned with where we have been as He is with where we are going. God is a God of deliverance who has paid a supreme price for our health. He has given us, as believers, the authority to defeat the enemy's plan against our health. But we cannot defeat what we embrace. If we embrace the enemy, we forfeit our authority to be redeemed from it. Walking in health is a kingdom truth that we must embrace if we are to defeat the enemy that wants to rob us of our redemptive right in Christ.

A Change of Mind

As my mind was renewed to embrace the promise of health and strength, I began to think differently. I set my mind on the things above, where God is (Col. 3:1). Then my success was not determined by the people around me but by the God who was in me. I was able to hold every thought captive rather than every thought (especially about food and exercise) holding me captive. I had been captive to weakness and poor health by the thought of foods that I knew were not good for me. Now I began to think thoughts of health and walk into freedom from my captivity.

For example, I knew the truth of God's Word declared, "For as he thinks within himself, so he is" (Prov. 23:7). So I knew that since I needed a change in my body, I was going to have a change in my thoughts. I had to overcome those old mind-sets of food and exercise that brought negative forces against me. I began to find new strength in speaking faith for my healing to "[destroy] speculations and every lofty thing raised up against the knowledge of God, and... [take] every thought captive to the obedience of Christ" (2 Cor. 10:5).

The enemy will use anything he can to destroy us. He brings sickness and causes our health to fail in order to get us to believe in what he does rather than in what God does. The "lofty things" that I raised against the knowledge of God focused on my desire for food rather than health. Isn't it the knowledge of God (truth) that sets us free? The enemy had me focusing on unhealthy living. He did not want my mind to be focused on God's truth about my health. His goal was to lift up my desire for unhealthy foods rather than my desire for God. He knew an unhealthy lifestyle would kill me and that a healthy lifestyle would heal me.

I began to use the divine weapons God gives us to defeat his destructive powers. The Word of God says "the weapons of our warfare are not of the flesh, but divinely powerful for the destruction of fortresses" (2 Cor. 10:4). Only by embracing and declaring the Word of God could I be set free from the stronghold the enemy was bringing. If the enemy can cause us to focus on the desires of the flesh, then our focus will not be on the Spirit of God who dwells in us and delivers us from the flesh. I had to experience a change of mind and set my mind upon my teacher, the Holy Spirit: "The Holy Spirit...will teach you all things, and bring to your remembrance all that I said to you" (John 14:26).

As truth came to my heart and mind, speculations from the enemy were brought down and my mind was renewed to health. I began to realize how freely the things of God could come to me as I yielded to the Holy Spirit: "Now we have received, not the spirit of the world, but the Spirit who is from God, so that we might *know* the things freely given to us by God" (1 Cor. 2:12, emphasis added). God wants us to know He freely has given health to us. To walk in that truth, we must cast down those lofty things the enemy is trying to cause us to embrace. The enemy is determined to steal our inheritance that we have from God. The problem I was having was that I gave the enemy my attention. When you pay attention to him, it will cost you.

All things are put under the feet of Jesus (1 Cor. 15:27). That means that, since we are members of the body of Christ, the devil is under our feet. My mind has been renewed with this truth, and now my attitude is that I need a full-time God to keep me from the destructions of the devil. I have determined to focus all my attention on my God, to be fully occupied by the Holy Spirit, in order to walk in the freedom He has promised in every area of my life.

Chapter 5

PARTNERING WITH THE HOLY SPIRIT

What you allow the Holy Spirit to do in you
determines what the Holy Spirit can do for you.

The key to your success on any kingdom endeavor is your partnering with the Holy Spirit. This is especially important regarding walking in health. I want to encourage you in your relationship with the Holy Spirit, showing what the Scriptures teach He will do supernaturally for you.

Divine "Occupation"

As I have discussed, when you are born again, you become a new creation as the Spirit of God comes to indwell your spirit and make you His temple. As you yield to His working within you, to the fullness of His "occupation" in your temple, He transforms you into the image of Christ. When you receive His power by faith, your body that has been subject to sickness will be changed into a body totally redeemed from sickness. As I mentioned earlier, when God "occupies" a believer, He fills you with His fullness, giving you the power of God within to set you free from sickness.

You are not filled with the Spirit of God to have to stand against sickness in your own power; you are empowered by the Holy Spirit to stand in God's power. There is nothing the devil has that can stand up against God's divine "occupation" of your spirit. The greater His occupation, the greater will be your power.

The more you yield to His control, the more freedom you will experience from the destructive power of the enemy. This is the true kingdom revelation you must begin to embrace in faith to be set free. Let me encourage you to read again the truth of God's Word regarding your relationship to the Holy Spirit:

> Do you not know that you are a temple of God and that the Spirit of God *dwells* in you? If any man destroys the temple of God, God will destroy him, for the temple of God is *holy*, and that is what you are.
>
> —1 Corinthians 3:16–17, emphasis added

"That is what you are": the temple of God. God's temple is not a building; it is a person—you. Because God occupies His temple, the temple is holy. To be *holy* is to be "pure, clean, and perfect."[1] I think we have a hard time receiving this truth because of "wrong filters" in our thinking. If we filter the Word of God through a fallen nature mindset, we think we have a life apart from God. That makes it difficult to understand how your physical body can be a holy temple. The determining factor for whether or not a believer is fully occupied with the Spirit of God lies in the will of man.

Your choice must be to allow the Spirit of God to fully occupy your temple. As I said earlier, this is true because God created man to walk in relationship with Him *willingly*, in love to choose Him above all else. I do not believe it is the will of God that a God-occupied believer also be occupied by the destructive power of the enemy. How can you be free from the enemy's power? The apostle Paul tells you how he lived in victory over him:

> I have been crucified with Christ; and it is no longer I who live, but Christ lives in me; and the life which I now live in the flesh I live by faith in the Son of God, who loved me and gave Himself up for me.
>
> —Galatians 2:20

As you declare this spiritual reality, you will begin to realize that you don't have a life apart from God. Your new life is in Christ, indwelling you by the power of the Holy Spirit; your life is over. And His Spirit is *holy*. It seems too good to be true. I had a hard time receiving this wonderful truth for my life.

Then the Holy Spirit said to me, "Why are you having a hard time letting go of a life that was not working?" I made a decision to let go of that life that had been "crucified with Christ." When I no longer live in my fallen nature mind-set, then Christ lives His life through me and I am a member of the body of Christ. There is a whole lot of freedom waiting for us when we choose to trade lives. Paul said, "...the life which I *now* live in the flesh"; he was not talking about a future life. We don't have to live in the flesh under the curse if we embrace the truth by faith that Christ lives in us.

Jesus taught this truth when He said: "Abide in Me, and I in you" (John 15:4). As believers, we live a life that is not ours. It is the life of Christ that cleanses us from *all* unrighteousness. The apostle Paul explained:

> For indeed He was crucified because of weakness, yet He lives because of the power of God. For we also are weak in Him, yet we will live with Him because of the power of God directed toward you.
>
> —2 Corinthians 13:4

How can this *not* be a healthy life? Allowing your life to be filled by divine occupation of the Holy Spirit gives you what you have not had: "the power of God directed toward you." When God fully indwells a believer, that believer will not be lacking in anything that God has promised. I thought when I got saved I had a life. I did not know that being saved meant my life was over. Now I have discovered it is a lot easier to allow Him to live His life through me. When I live in His life, my life becomes full of blessing and health. The Spirit of God abides in us to fulfill the will of God for us. We simply have to hear what the Spirit is saying as we learn to walk with Him:

> But I say, walk by the Spirit, and you will not carry out the desire of the flesh. For the flesh sets its desire against the Spirit, and the Spirit against the flesh.
>
> —GALATIANS 5:16–17

Your flesh-life may try to assert itself against the life of the Spirit within you. But as you choose to walk by the Spirit, your flesh or carnal mind will lose its power over your desires. According to the Scriptures, the problem is placing your desires on the flesh and not on the life of God indwelling you by His Spirit. When you submit to God so that you are fully occupied with His Spirit, He will go before you to prepare the way so that your past failure will no longer overtake your future.

A Spiritual House

Partnering with the Holy Spirit will build up your *spirit man*—the real *you*. The Holy Spirit occupies your spirit so that you become a spiritual house and can be strengthened and established in the things of God. The apostle Jude admonished believers, "But you, beloved, building yourselves up on your most holy faith, praying in the Holy Spirit" (Jude 20). Communing with God by the power of the Spirit develops your spirit man and strengthens your faith.

Because God is spirit and you are created in the image of God, you are created as a spirit man or woman. That is who you are. When Adam sinned, he died spiritually to relationship with God, and his mind began to rule his life instead of his spirit. When you are born again, your spirit is made alive to God through redemption, and His Spirit indwells your spirit.

But the apostle Paul understood that at salvation, your carnal mind is not automatically renewed to think God's thoughts. That is why you must learn to listen to the Spirit of God, receive the Word of God, and chose to walk by the Spirit, allowing your "old man," your flesh, to be crucified with Christ.

When the mind is in charge, it will always set itself on desires of the flesh and the world's order of things. God created us to be a spirit man, to live in a physical body, and to have an intellect or mind. Through redemption, our spirit man needs to be built up by the Spirit of God teaching us how to walk with Him. The Holy Spirit teaches the spirit of man by renewing the mind of man according to the Word of God and restoring health to the body of man.

The apostle Peter wrote of this spiritual transformation: "You also, as living stones, are being built up as a spiritual house for a holy priesthood…" (1 Pet. 2:5). The body of Christ, which is a *spiritual* body, is made up of believers whose *physical* bodies are fully occupied by and governed by the Spirit of God.

As a Spirit-led man or woman, you will walk in liberty. Scripture teaches that, "Where the Spirit of the Lord is, there is liberty" (2 Cor. 3:17). It is in this liberty that believers can do all things through Christ, who strengthens them (Phil. 4:13). That includes living in a spiritual house that is free from all bondage and sickness.

We Will Receive Power

As we learn to become fully occupied by the Holy Spirit, we receive all that the Spirit of God embodies. The Holy Spirit does not simply *bring* divine power; He *is* divine power. The Creator is all powerful, as is revealed through Creation. When God shows up, you will experience His divine power: "You will receive power when the Holy Spirit has come upon you" (Acts 1:8). This does not mean you will have more power. It means you will have His power. The power of the Holy Spirit comes not only to teach you but to protect you as well: "Who are protected by the power of God through faith..." (1 Pet. 1:5).

Remember, it is your faith, your trust in God, that activates the protection of God's armor for believers. If you are the vehicle, the power of God is the driving force. It takes the driving force of God's power in you to maintain momentum against the enemy's power. To walk in health is not an on-again-off-again proposition. It is a continual lifestyle of healthy choices, which requires the power of God to maintain. When I thought I could walk this journey of health in my own strength, I failed over and over. How many people are trying to be healthy by following all kinds of diet and exercise programs in their own strength and failing as I did? That is why we are fast becoming a nation with a pandemic of obesity and sickness.

To avert this disaster, as believers we must begin to realize how much God wants to help us to become healthy, whole people. He promises to supply all our needs: "And my God will supply all your needs according to His riches in glory in Christ Jesus" (Phil. 4:19). The Holy Spirit dwelling in us fully has the power to supply all our needs, not just some of our needs. When we have a need to become healthy and strong, God will supply the strength by His power, motivating us and giving us the ability to endure to achieve it. The Holy Spirit will enable us to keep going and not quit when things seem tough:

> Therefore, do not throw away your confidence, which has a great reward. For you have need of endurance, so that when you have done the will of God, you may receive what was promised.
> —HEBREWS 10:35–36

As we walk by faith into health, the Word of God encourages us not to throw our confidence away; that confidence will give us the reward of health we are looking for. But we must develop endurance so that when we have done the will of God, we will have the promise.

The Greek word for *endurance* means "to be consistently constant, not wavering when trials come."[2] It is translated as "patience" in the King James Version. When I began to exercise, I needed God's strength to help me develop endurance to be consistent at it. I cannot tell you how many times I wanted to quit. I began to understand that failure is easy; success is hard. I needed the power of the Holy Spirit to give me endurance. With endurance came confidence, and growing with confidence, I eventually received the prize of a strong body. With God all things are truly possible.

It is comforting to know that we are simply earthen vessels that contain the supernatural power of God: "But we have this treasure in earthen vessels, so that the surpassing greatness of the power will be of God and not from ourselves" (2 Cor. 4:7). When we yield our vessel to God, He deposits His wealth within us, the surpassing greatness of the power of God. This is our guarantee for success. Without God, I can fail; with God, I succeed. The goal of succeeding is that "the life of Jesus also may be manifested in our mortal flesh" (v. 11).

As born-again believers, we are the body of Christ in the earth. Through His redemption His life changes our life and is manifested in our mortal flesh. We are to glorify God in our body, to show forth all the benefits that the cross has provided. We are not to show forth the things we have been delivered from; we are to show forth the things we have been delivered unto in health and wholeness. The life of Jesus was not being manifested in my mortal body when I was unhealthy and sick. We must understand what the life of Jesus doesn't simply deliver us *from* the darkness of sin and sickness; His life delivers us *into* freedom and wholeness:

> He delivered us from the power of darkness and conveyed us into the kingdom of the Son of His love.
>
> —COLOSSIANS 1:13, NKJV

We are not just taken out of darkness; we have a new citizenship in the kingdom of Christ. We are not only delivered from something, but we are also delivered into something. For example, we are delivered from the curse of sickness from which we have been redeemed. There is no sickness in Christ. We are transferred into kingdom of light. This tells me that I have the authority, by the power of God, to walk in health with strength. This kingdom of God that I have been delivered into "does not consist in words but in power" (1 Cor. 4:20).

The Anointing

Understanding the anointing of the Holy Spirit gives clarity to why we must partner with Him. The anointing is the expression of true partnership. The goal of God is not just to occupy us fully by His Spirit, but to transform us into the image of His Son. The anointing of the Holy Spirit is that transforming power. The Greek word for *anointing*[3] refers to smearing or rubbing ointment (in the Old Testament, the anointing oil) and through that to be endowed with supernatural power. In other words, the anointing is an endowment of the very characteristics, qualities, and virtues of the Holy Spirit dwelling within us. These divine qualities are meant to change us from who we are into the divine character of who God is in us.

It is the anointing of the Holy Spirit that brings a transformation in the believer. When you come in contact with the anointing, it does not change your *moment*; it changes your whole life. It is designed to cause you to never be the same. The anointing destroys the yoke of bondage because it is the power of God in you to deliver you. The prophet Isaiah declared this wonderful promise regarding the anointing of God:

> And it shall come to pass in that day, that his burden shall be taken away from off thy shoulder, and his yoke from off thy neck, and the yoke shall be destroyed because of the anointing.
>
> —ISAIAH 10:27, KJV

The Holy Spirit endows us with His divine anointing to assimilate us into the body of Christ, never to be separated from Him. Remember, we are not only individual vessels of the Holy Spirit but also the body of Christ. As the body of Christ we are the representation of Christ, who is the head of His body, the church. Therefore, as redeemed people, the goal of the Holy Spirit's anointing is to conform us into the image of Jesus:

> For those whom He foreknew, He also predestined to become conformed to the image of His Son, so that He would be the first-born among many brethren.
> —ROMANS 8:29

While that is God's plan, it is up to us to be willing to receive the anointing. We have to humble ourselves, give up our independence, and become inter-independent with God: "Therefore humble yourselves under the mighty hand of God, that He may exalt you at the proper time" (1 Pet. 5:6). When would be a proper time to be exalted? Maybe when you need a breakthrough in your health, finances, marriage, or any other area of your life. I think any believer who chooses to live under the mighty hand of God will live an exalted life. Because the anointing is the divine nature of God experienced by man, when we submit to it we have everything we need to be victorious in life:

> Seeing that His divine power has granted to us everything pertaining to life and godliness, through the true knowledge of Him who called us by His own glory and excellence. For by these He has granted to us His precious and magnificent promises, so that by them you may become partakers of the divine nature...
> —2 PETER 1:3–4

It is the anointing that provides the power for us to walk in life and godliness. His "precious and magnificent" promises give us that life so we can become partakers of God's divine nature. To have the anointing is to have a continual encounter with the Spirit of God.

Our Teacher

We need to partner with the Holy Spirit because He is our Teacher. Jesus promised His disciples that when He returned to His Father, He would send them a Helper, the Holy Spirit, who "will teach you all things" (John 14:26). He also called Him the "Spirit of truth" (v. 17). God wants us to know His truth because it is in knowing truth that the will of God can be fulfilled in our lives. As our Helper, the Holy Spirit reveals divine truth to us: "But you have an anointing from the Holy One, and you all *know*" (1 John 2:20, emphasis added).

Your mind is renewed by knowing truth and embracing it. The apostle John went on to declare that the Holy Spirit teaches you all things (v. 27), reiterating the words of Jesus. It is the anointing that witnesses to your spirit the knowledge of truth. This is really important to understand. There is a war going on in the minds of believers, caused by the enemy desiring that you be conformed to the world. When a believer is weighed down by sickness, poverty, conflict, and other grievous problems, there is a tendency to allow these negative situations to "teach you" rather than allowing the Holy Spirit to teach you.

The apostle Paul warned believers not to be conformed to the world. When your thoughts are conformed to the world's thoughts, your mind-set tells you that God's Word must not mean what it says because you don't see it happening in your life. There is a tendency to bring the Word down to the level of your experience rather than allowing the Holy Spirit to bring your experience up to the level of the Word. Truth is designed to set you free, not leave you in bondage to the mind-set of the world.

You cannot really know truth without receiving it from your Teacher, through the anointing of the Holy Spirit. It is the anointing that puts the revelation of truth in your spirit and causes you to recognize, "This is God." Without the anointing to *know*, you will conform to your condition and justify it with, "This is just how it is." I know, because that is what I used to do.

I was in a battle for the sanity of my mind. I was in such bad physical and mental shape that I thought, "Well, why bother to change?" Most people around me seemed to think the same way. I knew I had received the Holy Spirit, but I did not have an anointing to *know* the truth that would set me free.

It was like the Holy Spirit was tanked up inside me. I was like a reservoir for the Holy Spirit rather than allowing Him to be a river of life flowing out of me. I did not realize that in relating to the Holy Spirit, there is a difference between being a reservoir and a river. So I lived in frustration, questioning why the Word said one thing but in my life I was experiencing another.

New eyes and ears

When I humbled myself and yielded to the Holy Spirit in totality, I said, "Take over my spirit, my mind, and my body. What I have been doing has not worked well." It did not take me long to figure out that in surrendering to God, I had nothing to be worried about. Maybe He was going to tell me something I *did* want to hear. I had served in the church for twenty-five years; I thought I knew it all.

Then the Holy Spirit asked me, "Why are you limiting God by what you think? If you pursue the mind of Christ, you will become unlimited by what He thinks." I remembered the scripture that says, "For who has known the mind of the Lord, that he will instruct Him? But we have the mind of Christ" (1 Cor. 2:16). The apostle Paul is speaking about our faith not resting on the wisdom of men but on the power of God (v. 5). I continued to read about a wisdom that comes from God that is not of this age and that the Spirit of God reveals it to us (v. 10). He said those things to be revealed are:

> Things which eye has not seen and ear has not heard, and which have not entered the heart of man, all that God has prepared for those who love Him.
>
> —1 CORINTHIANS 2:9

When I had read this passage in the past, I thought, "This must be talking about things we will experience in heaven." Instead, now I saw that the Spirit of God reveals them to us living here on earth, in the present. Then Paul says that "we have received, not the spirit of the world, but the Spirit who is from God, so that we may *know* the things freely given to us by God" (v. 12, emphasis added). Because of the lack of anointing to *know*, I was missing the truth in God's Word that I had read many times. After surrendering totally to the Holy Spirit, it was as though a light came on in my spirit, illuminating the truth to me. He anointed my eyes to see the truth. I would read familiar verses and exclaim, "How did I miss that?"

I remembered the many years I had prepared a teaching for Sunday school when I would get out all my Bible translations and concordances and spend hours preparing the lesson. Yet when I taught the lesson, there seemed to be little response; it did not seem to go anywhere. Now, after the anointing of the Spirit was released through my humbling myself before Him, I was just driving down the street and pulling over to jot down on a notepad what I was hearing the Spirit say. I had been given new spiritual eyes to see and ears to hear God's truth. (Note: An advantage here is that it does not take hours to hear what the Spirit is saying. He will cause the Word to be living and active in our hearts.)

I began to realize that God has no limitations. He has things to give us that our eyes have not seen and our ears have not heard. As

I learn to partner with the Holy Spirit, the revelation of these things will come to me through His Word; His Word is truth (John 17:17). His divine revelation will teach us that the Word of God is the will of God. Through His will we are to know Him.

Knowing God is not limited to understanding words in a book. Every author is greater than what he or she writes. God's Word is creative, because, as John stated so beautifully, "In the beginning was the Word, and the Word was with God, and the Word was God" (John 1:1). The Scriptures declare that the Word of God is "living and active and sharper than any two-edged sword, and piercing as far as the division of soul and spirit..." (Heb. 4:12). As we embrace His Word and declare its truth, God Himself will create the redemptive reality we speak. We can only worship Him as we say that knowing God "is almost too wonderful for words."

Revelation of the Supernatural Realm

The Spirit of God is in us to make us supernatural. That is, a Spirit-filled believer, when yielded to the Holy Spirit, becomes "super" natural, or more than natural. We cannot even understand the supernatural realm from a natural perspective. The apostle Paul wrote: "But a natural man does not accept the things of the Spirit of God, for they are foolishness to him; and he cannot understand them, because they are spiritually appraised" (1 Cor. 2:14).

When we become a new creation and a temple for the Holy Spirit, we become a spiritual person. We are born again and are made alive to God, who is spirit. He dwells in a supernatural realm and infuses our lives—body, soul, and spirit—with His supernatural power. What limitations does God encounter in a yielded vessel? We have more potential for bringing His will to the earth as it is done in heaven than we give ourselves credit for; we need to learn to embrace the power of God within us.

As believers, it is important that we become familiar with this heavenly supernatural realm of which we are citizens. If we do not, we have a tendency to maintain a separation in our minds, living natural lives as we did before we were born again. Then we cannot believe what Jesus taught us to pray, that God's kingdom is meant to come on the earth; His will is to be done here as it is in heaven.

It is not God's will that heaven and earth be separated, out of harmony and having different goals and purposes. If you think about it, the natural realm became an expression of the supernatural realm in Creation. God, who is supernatural, spoke the natural realm into existence; what was unseen became seen. And when Jesus came, His purpose was to unite us to God once again, to bring the kingdom of God to earth. He came to restore the *natural* to its proper relationship with the *supernatural*. When the will of God is fulfilled in the natural realm, the supernatural and the natural become one as God intended.

Choosing between two kingdoms

Of course, the devil, the enemy of our souls, also dwells in a supernatural realm—the realm of darkness. When we experience sickness and confront it with the Spirit of God, there is a collision of two kingdoms: The supernatural kingdom of God (light) impacts the supernatural kingdom of the enemy (darkness). In that collision the power of God reorders the natural, bringing healing as the will of God is fulfilled. Divine revelation of truth reveals the supernatural realm to us so that we can see the will of God and discern the plans of the enemy.

The kingdom of God cannot come to earth if it is not revealed in us and through us. Supernatural vision will cause us to see life in the kingdom of God. When that happens, God's supernatural realm can be seen in the natural. In other words, the natural becomes supernatural when God shows up through us. His divine power overrules the natural as well as the enemy's supernatural forces of darkness.

Becoming familiar with the supernatural realm involves yielding fully to the Holy Spirit, who is the supernatural power of God dwelling within us, as I have discussed. He makes supernatural things happen through us. He wants to work with us for the fulfillment of God's will and purposes in the earth:

> God also testifying with them, both by signs and wonders and by various miracles and by gifts of the Holy Spirit according to His own will.
>
> —HEBREWS 2:4

This verse reveals the divine partnership, which we have discussed—God, by the Holy Spirit, testifying with them. This is God backing up His own Word with signs, wonders, and miracles. He is working through believers by the power of the Holy Spirit in the supernatural realm. It is difficult to experience supernatural events if you are not familiar with the supernatural realm. And it is difficult to gain victory over the enemy's lies if you don't discern his schemes by the power of the Holy Spirit. The apostle Paul declared of the devil: "We are not ignorant of his schemes" (2 Cor. 2:11). How can you defeat a spirit enemy unless you become a godly spirit person?

The purpose of divine revelation is to make God's will clear to us so that we can fulfill His will in our lives. Revelation reveals truth, truth establishes faith, and faith is the substance of what we are hoping for. The apostle Paul prayed, "That the God of our Lord Jesus Christ, the Father of glory, may give to you a spirit of wisdom and of revelation in the knowledge of Him" (Eph. 1:17). The spirit of revelation comes to reveal the Person of God the Father and Christ Jesus so that we can walk in the supernatural realm in knowledge of God.

I have encountered Christians who were afraid of the supernatural realm. When we fear anything of the Spirit realm, it is an indication we are not walking as we should with the Holy Spirit. He gives us an anointing to know all things. Learning to walk in God's supernatural power gives us God's ability to walk in divine health. If we set our mind on the things above, not on the things on earth (Col. 3:2), we will begin to enter into all that God has prepared for us to receive for life. The anointing He gives us provides gifts of the Spirit and fruit of the Spirit to know the difference between what is from God and what is from the enemy. Without this supernatural anointing we cannot know the difference. We cannot embrace everything that is supernatural without knowing from which kingdom it comes, the kingdom of light or the kingdom of darkness. For example, I have heard some Christians embrace sickness and say they are sick for God's glory. Sickness does not come from the kingdom of God; it emanates from the kingdom of darkness.

God's Word tells us, "...that the Father may be glorified in the Son [what He has done]" (John 14:13). Jesus does not make us sick. He commanded His disciples to "heal the sick" (Matt. 10:8). He did not say, "Make people sick so that God would be glorified." The Father is glorified by what the Son has done in bringing healing to the sick. He is not glorified in what the devil has done to make us sick. The Father sent His Son to deliver us, not bring us into bondage. He came to destroy the works of the evil one (1 John 3:8) and to glorify His Father. That is why we must embrace the exhortation of the apostle Paul: "For you have been bought with a price: therefore glorify God in your body" (1 Cor. 6:20).

We can get all this mixed up when we are not familiar with the supernatural realm of the Spirit. It is difficult to receive a healing from God when we think the sickness we are trying to get delivered from is OK with God. When we think God allowed it, we cannot think God wants to take it away. God does not allow His children to be sick for His glory or to "teach them something." The goal of the enemy is to bring sickness to the body of Christ; he must rejoice when God's people wrongly ascribe that evil work to God. In doing so, they justify what the enemy does and deny the will of God to bring healing and wholeness to their life.

Fulfilling the Will of God

The power to fulfill the will of God comes by the Spirit of God working through our lives. The Spirit of God is in us specifically for that fulfillment. Our relationship with the Holy Spirit determines whether or not that fulfillment can take place. As I mentioned, this spiritual reality is not about a natural man having a relationship with the Spirit of God. The natural man cannot fulfill God's will or even understand it. We discussed the fact that the things of God do not make sense to the natural man (1 Cor. 2:14). The natural man focuses on natural "reality" and cannot understand kingdom reality. When the natural man tries to do the works of God, it results in dead works (Heb. 9:14). Religious spirits motivate the natural man, bringing forth a form of godliness but denying its power (2 Tim. 3:5). Where a supernatural, spiritual relationship with Christ is void, this spirit of religion will exist.

The natural man cannot accept the things of the Spirit because they are spiritually appraised or discerned. A Christian who does not partner with the Holy Spirit will not understand the supernatural realm. The natural man has no spiritual discernment. Without discernment, we cannot understand and, therefore, will not accept the spiritual reality of the Spirit; it appears as foolishness to the natural mind. To the natural man, what the Holy Spirit reveals is considered absurd; it does not make sense. The natural man does not embrace supernatural signs, wonders, miracles, healings, and health; a spiritual man who is yielded to the Holy Spirit will receive them. Partnering with the Holy Spirit gives us God's ability to become the fulfillment of His Word.

Reveals the Mind of Christ

The apostle Paul declares in 1 Corinthians 2:16, "We have the mind of Christ." Spiritual discernment will reveal what is in the mind of Jesus. If we are His body and He is our head, shouldn't we have his mind? Having the mind of Christ means to understand the supernatural realm. The Holy Spirit dwells in us as our Teacher so that we can understand what is on the mind of Christ. When Paul quotes the prophet's words regarding the things God has prepared for those who love Him (1 Cor. 2:9), he concludes:

> For to us God revealed them through the Spirit; for the Spirit searches all things, even the depths of God.
>
> —1 CORINTHIANS 2:10

What is God revealing to us through the Spirit? He is revealing supernatural realities of His kingdom so that we can receive them. With the mind of Christ, we are to know what God wants to give us.

> Now we have received, not the spirit of the world, but the Spirit who is from God, so that we may know the things freely given to us by God.
>
> —1 CORINTHIANS 2:12

Isn't this interesting? The Spirit searches all things, even the depths of God, and we have received that same Spirit. Why? So that we can know what is on the mind of Christ. It is by this supernatural revelation that we have understanding that allows us to receive what God freely gives. We short-circuit this divine process when we are afraid to embrace the fullness of the Holy Spirit and yield our lives totally to Him. When we have the mind of Christ, our mind becomes like a divine computer that stores what God tells us in our renewed memory bank.

He Gifts Us

Partnering with the Holy Spirit provides spiritual gifts that become operational in our lives. The gifts of the Holy Spirit are supernatural tools that we activate according to the will of God. This impartation of divine power begins when we are baptized into the body of Christ:

> Repent, and each of you be baptized in the name of Jesus Christ for the forgiveness of your sins; and you will receive the *gift* of the Holy Spirit.
>
> —ACTS 2:38, EMPHASIS ADDED

Too many Christians receive their new spiritual life when they are born again, but they do not have a proper understanding of the spiritual gifts the Holy Spirit offers them; therefore they have no victory. It is in understanding the divine power the Holy Spirit brings that determines whether or not we live in victory. When we value the Holy Spirit's presence in our lives, we become winners. Instead of living with a loser's mentality, battling daily for victory, we view life from God's perspective of present victory. Throughout the race of life, not just when we cross the finish line, we understand that "greater is He who is in you than he who is in the world" (1 John 4:4). We don't have to battle *for* the victory against our foes; we battle *from* the victory that Christ won for us. When the apostle Paul listed tribulation, distress, persecution, famine, and many other threats to our Christian lives, he concluded:

> But in all these things we overwhelmingly conquer through Him who loved us.
>
> —ROMANS 8:37

We overwhelmingly conquer every challenge of the evil one because greater is He who is in us than he who comes against us. Jesus said that He has given His disciples authority over all the power of the enemy (Luke 10:19). As we yield to the power of the Holy Spirit, we will increasingly exhibit that authority. When I realized this source of divine power, I began to pay attention to the gifts of the Holy Spirit, desiring that they be released through me. I understood that I was weak when I neglected the supernatural power He had made available to me.

Paul exhorted the young minister Timothy: "Do not neglect the spiritual gift within you" (1 Tim. 4:14). When we neglect the gifts of the Holy Spirit, we lack the supernatural tools that bring about the will of God in our lives. I needed these tools to become healthy and strong. I had to stir up the spiritual gifts (2 Tim. 1:6, KJV) within me and apply them in my everyday life. The spirit man must energize the natural man. Partnering with the Holy Spirit brings restoration to the "earthen vessel," His temple, so that it can be a vehicle for the supernatural life of God to flow through. The gifts of the Spirit not only transform and empower our own life, but they will also transform and empower others as we do the work of the ministry. Let's look at one list of spiritual gifts that are available to us:

> Now there are varieties of gifts, but the same Spirit. And there are varieties of ministries, and the same Lord. And there are varieties of effects, but the same God who works all things in all persons. But to each one is given the manifestation of the Spirit for the common good. For to one is given the word of wisdom through the Spirit, and to another the word of knowledge according to the same Spirit; to another faith by the same Spirit, and to another the gifts of healing by one Spirit, and to another the effecting of miracles, and to another prophecy, and to another the distinguishing of spirits, to another various kinds of tongues, and to another the interpretation of tongues. But one and the same Spirit works all these things, distributing to each one individually just as He wills.
>
> —1 CORINTHIANS 12:4–11

The apostle Paul writes about *spiritual gifts, ministries,* and *effects* that are available to us through the Spirit of God. These charismatic gifts are available for the ministries Jesus calls us to fulfill, resulting in supernatural effects or workings by the Spirit of God through us. Everyone has spiritual gifts, ministries, and effects available to them. Jesus calls us to ministry, the Holy Spirit brings the gifts for the ministry, and the effect is to fulfill God's will on the earth. Believers are given various manifestations of the Spirit for the good of all. The gifts of the Spirit are not just for somebody; they are for the building up of the church, His body.

The nine gifts of the Spirit listed here can be categorized into three areas: utterance gifts, power gifts, and revelation gifts. Gifts of prophecy, diverse kinds of tongues, and the interpretation of tongues are gifts of *utterance* or speaking. The *power* gifts are the gift of faith, working of miracles, and gifts of healing. And the *revelation* gifts include the word of knowledge, word of wisdom, and the discerning of spirits.

The value of the utterance gifts is that they speak what the Holy Spirit is saying, for example, regarding God's will for your health. The power gifts release supernatural faith for healing and miracles. And the revelation gifts reveal the truth of God that exposes the enemy's lies so that you can know it is God's will for you to walk in health. The Holy Spirit works all these things according to His will (v. 11).

The apostle Paul instructed believers to earnestly desire the greater gifts (v. 30). And Jesus said the Father desires to give His children good gifts to those who ask for them (Matt. 7:11). When you embrace the gift of the Holy Spirit, you have in you all that the Holy Spirit has made available for the abundant life Christ promised. The gifts of the Holy Spirit provide the power for every believer to achieve divine health and walk in it.

Fruit of the Spirit

The fruit of the Spirit grows in the life of us as believers, transforming our character into the character of Christ by the power of the Spirit within us. As we choose to walk in the Spirit, allowing Him to fully occupy His temple, He changes us from who we are to who He is:

> But the fruit of the Spirit is love, joy, peace, patience, kindness, goodness, faithfulness, gentleness, self-control; against such things there is no law.
>
> —GALATIANS 5:22–23

When we yield to the Holy Spirit, the endowment of the anointing of the Spirit results in a life filled with the fruit of the Spirit. We are restored into the image and likeness of God, who is love (1 John 4:8). As we become the body of Christ in the earth, the fruit of the Spirit reflects His image. Jesus's character is love, joy, peace, patience, kindness, goodness, faithfulness, gentleness, and self-control. It is our destiny to be conformed to the image of Christ (Rom. 8:29).

It is the fruit of the Spirit—godly character—that empowers the gifts of the Spirit. Without the fruit, the gifts become corrupted. It is the counterfeit that brings corruption. For example, the counterfeit of love is hatred. It is the fruit of love that releases healing; it is hatred that corrupts it. The joy of the Lord is your strength (Neh. 8:10); the counterfeit of joy is depression, which steals your strength. The enemy's goal is to steal the spiritual fruit from the lives of believers by replacing it with the counterfeit. In healing rooms, we see so many people who come for prayer because they have bought into the counterfeit lie of the enemy.

The apostle Paul declares of the fruit of the Spirit, "…against such there is no law" (Gal. 5:23, KJV). In other words, nothing can contradict the power of love or the character of Christ. Paul reminds believers that the fruit of the Spirit grows in a life that has "crucified the flesh with its passions and desires" (v. 24). If we choose to live by the Spirit, we will walk in the Spirit and be transformed into the image of Christ. Then the passions and desires of our flesh will no longer rule over us. I think this includes our passions and desires for unhealthy foods that result in unhealthy bodies, subject to obesity, diabetes, blocked arteries, heart attacks, and other destructive forces. We can live by the Spirit and walk by the Spirit as we choose to yield continually to His power and presence that indwell us.

Our Protection

Walking with the Holy Spirit gives us divine protection. In the natural, we hire a security guard because we need protection. In the kingdom, God sends His Spirit, who gives us security in the spirit realm. The Spirit of God provides the power to overcome our enemy. Jesus declared:

> Upon this rock I will build My church; and the gates of Hades [hell] will not overpower it.
>
> —MATTHEW 16:18

The New Testament teaches that Christ is the cornerstone of God's household, which is built "on the foundation of the apostles and prophets" (Eph. 2:20). This strong foundation for the church will support God's people so that the gates of hell will not overpower them. God provides His divine protection when we choose to live upon His rock Christ Jesus. You could say that God is our spiritual security guard. The household of God protects us from the destructive plans of the enemy. That is why it is so important to be a part of the body of Christ. We are not to be outside looking in; we are to be inside looking out.

The church has been given the keys of the kingdom of God to help believers walk in victory and fulfill the will of God in the earth. Jesus declared:

> I will give you the keys of the kingdom of heaven; and whatever you bind on earth shall have been bound in heaven, and whatever you shall loose on earth shall have been loosed in heaven.
>
> —MATTHEW 16:19

We have protection when we live inside the house of God, not outside of it. Too many Christians believe this scripture means we only have *access* to the kingdom of God, meaning we are outside trying to get in. But Jesus said we have the keys *of* the kingdom. As God's household of faith, we have been given keys to open every door and authority to bind and loose on earth. From that position of divine access to the Father we can be victorious over every foe: "For through Him we both have our access in one Spirit to the Father" (Eph. 2:18).

In the kingdom of God He becomes our refuge, our safe place: "The rock of my strength, my refuge is in God" (Ps. 62:7). Again, kingdom protection is not determined by what we see in the natural; it is determined by what we believe. Our protection is from our God, who is spirit, against the enemy, who is also spirit. Protection is spiritually discerned as we exercise our faith:

> For our struggle is not against flesh and blood, but against the rulers, against the powers, against the world forces of this darkness, against the spiritual forces of wickedness in the heavenly places.
>
> —EPHESIANS 6:12

A natural man cannot battle against spiritual forces of the enemy's kingdom. By the Spirit of God we are able to battle these demonic forces and defeat their diabolical plans. God knew this and gave us

His Spirit to provide a shield against the forces: "He is a shield to those who walk in integrity" (Prov. 2:7). The Hebrew word translated *integrity* means "upright, whole, living according to His will."[4] Divine protection is activated in our lives when our spirit partners with the Spirit of God. Without this partnership we lose our protection. When we obey God, He not only protects us from spiritual forces, but also He will even rebuke the enemy on our behalf. For example, in obeying God in giving tithes and offerings, He promises:

> "Test Me now in this," says the LORD of hosts, "if I will not open for you the windows of heaven and pour out for you a blessing until it overflows. Then I will rebuke the devourer for you, so that it will not destroy the fruits of the ground; nor will your vine in the field cast its grapes," says the LORD of hosts.
>
> —MALACHI 3:10–11

God is saying, "If you will obey My Word, you can test me and see that I will open up the windows of heaven in blessing your life. I will rebuke the devourer on your behalf." I call that divine protection. The prophet Isaiah declared God's divine defense, which is a heritage of the servants of the Lord: "No weapon that is formed against you will prosper" (Isa. 54:17). Again he declared: "Behold, the Lord GOD will help me; who is he that shall condemn me?" (Isa. 50:9, KJV).

When I needed help to overcome the enemy's attacks against my mind and body, I called on the Holy Spirit. He provided the power to win those battles in the realm of the spirit. Food had become an addiction in my life, just like drugs or anything else that takes control of us to destroy our lives. I discovered that divine partnership with the Holy Spirit provides supernatural protection from every destructive force. My partner, the Holy Spirit, who dwells is in me, gave me the power to overcome my addiction to unhealthy food.

Reveals the Kingdom of God

The Holy Spirit will reveal the kingdom of God to us. Jesus taught us to pray, "Thy kingdom come. Thy will be done in earth, as it is in heaven" (Matt. 6:10, KJV). When His kingdom comes to earth, His will is done in the earth. As believers, our mandate is to seek first, as our priority of life, the kingdom of God:

> But seek first His kingdom and His righteousness, and all these things will be added to you.
> —MATTHEW 6:33

Jesus promised that when we seek first His kingdom, He provides all we need for our lives on earth. That supernatural provision comes to earth as it is in heaven. If there is no sickness in heaven, there is not to be any sickness on earth. If we are to have health in heaven, we should have health on earth when we live in His kingdom grace. Only when we embrace the spiritual reality of His kingdom can we understand this. Our minds have to be renewed to kingdom possibilities, or they will be conformed to what look like "natural realities."

The kingdom of God comes to change the world, not justify it. This truth is established in the earth through believers yielding to the Spirit of God, partnering with Him to fulfill the will of God. We are to seek *first* His kingdom, not in times of trouble. That Greek word for *first* means "at the beginning, chiefly or foremost in our life."[5] Our provision for every area of life, as believers, comes from the kingdom of God. That is why it must become our priority of life to seek His kingdom.

Divine health is in the kingdom of God. When I did not seek first the kingdom, my provision was based on what man provided. I thought if I just accepted what the world provided, everything would be all right. After all, doesn't the world have my best interest in mind? I followed the crowd, living according to our culture. Anything at the grocery store was all right. I ate at fast-food restaurants just as everyone seemed to do. I thought if I had any problems, I could go to the doctor and get it fixed. After my heart attack, I realized that I could also get sick and die—like everyone else. I discovered that an unredeemed world did not have my interest in mind; they had their bottom line and selfish interests in mind.

Only when I sought God's kingdom and His righteousness did all the things I needed for health begin to be added to me. The Holy Spirit began to speak to me about seeking the kingdom of God. He said to me, "If you will understand the kingdom that Jesus came to establish in the earth, all you need in your life will be available to you." I thought, "How long is this going to take? I need help now. Can this all happen very quickly? Wow, I am in a mess. Can God come and fix me?" Then He said, "I don't want to fix you because I don't want to restore you to the way you have been living; I want to transform you so that you will be like I am in My kingdom. You are not going to be a man who has God; I'm going to be to you God who has a man."

The Holy Spirit then called my attention to the word *seek* in Matthew 6:33. The Greek word for *seek* means "to search for something hidden, to inquire, aim at, strive after, to crave."[6] I discovered I had to begin a journey of seeking for understanding that would move me out of the kingdom of man, with which I was very familiar, into the kingdom of God, with which I was not familiar. I wondered, "How can I know a kingdom that I cannot see?" The Holy Spirit responded kindly, "That's why I give you an anointing, so that you will know." He showed me the promise:

> To you it has been granted to know the mysteries of the kingdom of heaven, but to them it has not been granted.
> —MATTHEW 13:11

I discovered that I could not know the kingdom of God as long as I was relying upon people to whom it had not been granted. The Holy Spirit reveals the mysteries of the kingdom of God to believers in Christ. When I relied on natural reality that I could see, I experienced failure, and with failure came increasing disappointment. It is the enemy that wants to steal the life of God's kingdom of righteousness, peace, and joy from us (Rom. 14:17).

I considered other words that begin with *d-i-s: disease, disability, disgrace, disbelief, disunity.* I looked up the prefix *dis-* in the dictionary. It means "to do the opposite, deprive of."[7] In other words, instead of the ease of God, we suffer the opposite, dis-ease; instead of the ability of God, we experience dis-ability; instead of the grace of God, we are ashamed by dis-grace; instead of belief in God, we embrace dis-belief; instead of unity in God, we live in dis-unity. The enemy brings disappointment to steal our *divine* appointment. In short, when we set our minds on the things that are on earth, we get "dis-ed."

In these and other ways the enemy sidetracks us from living victoriously in the kingdom of God. We are so focused on the trauma of living in the natural world that we have no energy for seeking an unseen kingdom. The devil causes us to focus on what he is doing so that we cannot focus on what God wants to do for us and in us. It is no wonder the devil causes failure to "dis-" the church.

The key to defeating the enemy is to focus on God and not on the devil. In the natural, when you go to war, you face your enemy. In the kingdom of God, by seeking Him first, you do not face your enemy; you face your God. What you face is what you embrace. Then the Bible says, "Submit therefore to God. Resist the devil and he will flee from you" (James 4:7). When we submit to God, He gives us the power to resist the enemy. My attitude is this—with a full-time God, who needs a devil? When we live in the kingdom of God, we live in a place where the enemy has no access. Submitting to God is partnering with the Holy Spirit, who resides within us. He does not partner as a part-time visitor; He comes to inhabit His temple and live the life of Christ in us and through us. It is this divine habitation that gives us kingdom authority.

Chapter 6

KINGDOM AUTHORITY

When you are under His authority,
you can exercise all authority.

Our success in achieving and walking in health comes by our God-given authority. God, the author of authority, has given us His authority. When we are under His authority, we can walk in all authority, which is given to release God's divine power to destroy the work of the enemy.

I used to think this promise of God had something to do with my power. The truth is that the power is not ours; it is the power of the Spirit of God released through the life of a believer. Jesus declared:

> Behold, I have given you authority [power] to tread upon serpents and scorpions, and over all the power of the enemy, and nothing will injure you.
>
> —LUKE 10:19

What we have been given is the divine authority of the Holy Spirit dwelling within us. With the Holy Spirit we have the power to destroy the work of the enemy. This scripture says we have power over *all* the power of the enemy, not just some of it. It does not ever say the enemy has power over us. We have all power over the enemy because the power of God dwells in us.

Jesus used two different words for *power* in this verse, which are important for us to understand. The *power* He has given to us to overcome the enemy is translated "authority," which contains the ideas of power of choice, liberty, permission, right, privilege to exercise ability or strength we possess.[1] He has given us the right and the strength to overcome the enemy through His power within us when we choose to do so.

When Jesus spoke of the *power* of the enemy, he used the Greek word *dunamis*, which means "inherent power by virtue of its nature."[2] The divine *authority* you have is always to be used to overcome any *power* of the enemy. This is really important to understand. If your life is more impacted with the work of the enemy than the work of God, you will live without victory. You cannot exhibit power over the power of the enemy as long as the enemy has power over you.

The works of the enemy include pain, sickness, poverty of spirit, financial lack, or any other thing that he sends to steal your ability to live victoriously in the authority God has given you. Yet Jesus gave you authority to fulfill His will in destroying the works of the devil (1 John 3:8). This position of authority is difficult to maintain if you choose to believe the work of the enemy that is destroying you. You know you are weak in your own ability. When the devil attacks you with his destructive work, he tries to get you to focus on your weakness rather than on God's power. When you focus on your weakness, you justify the way you are rather than the way God has provided for your victory in living the abundant life (John 10:10).

When you recognize that the divine power you have is not yours, but rather God's power dwelling in you, you can choose to walk in His victory.

> But we have this treasure in earthen vessels, so that the surpassing greatness of the power will be of God and not from ourselves.
> —2 Corinthians 4:7

The way to our deliverance is always through the Deliverer. The enemy will always measure us by how we see ourselves. We need revelation to understand that we have God's power within us enabling us to live free of the work of the enemy. Our mind must be renewed to this biblical reality so that we know the power we have is not ours but God's. When we look away from our weakness to God's power within, the enemy will know that we know we have authority over his works in our life. By our knowing, we will enter into the fullness of authority.

Jesus promised, "Nothing will injure you" (Luke 10:19). Knowing the power of God that is in us helps us to put on the whole armor of God, lifting up the shield of faith to extinguish all the flaming missiles of the enemy (Eph. 6:13–17). Our God-given authority will allow us to enter into that place where nothing of the enemy can injure us. In this place of victory we walk in health; we are renewed to the truth that sets us free from sickness. In this place of freedom we are not afraid to believe in the promise of all things being possible with God, who dwells in us. This revelation gives us kingdom authority. It allows us to move higher in the knowledge of God so that the Word we read becomes the Word we live.

The Kingdom of God

It is not enough for us to know we have authority; we must understand God's purpose for giving it to us. As I have mentioned, Jesus came to restore to mankind the dominion that Adam and Eve lost when they fell to sin, disobeying God's commands. When we are restored to God through Christ's redemption, He gives us dominion (authority) once again. Jesus continually taught in parables regarding the kingdom of God and how to recognize it. From the beginning of His ministry, He began to declare, "Repent, for the kingdom of heaven is at hand" (Matt. 4:17).

The Greek word for *repent* means "to change one's mind for better, abhorring past sins." It carries the idea of turning from sin to God, restoring our position of right relationship with God.[3] Redemption restores the born-again Christian to a place of fellowship with the Father. We repent, and we are born again, becoming new creatures in Christ, as I discussed earlier. The Spirit of God enters into our re-created spirit, making us His temple. And we have the privilege of communing with the Holy Spirit, who becomes our divine Teacher.

Our new position in God is possible because the blood of Jesus has cleansed us from all unrighteousness. We are no longer separated from our heavenly Father by our sin; we are in Christ, "who became to us wisdom from God, and righteousness and sanctification, and redemption" (1 Cor. 1:30).

It was the kingdom of God that Jesus was bringing to earth, not simply healings, signs and wonders, or miracles. The kingdom of love brings all of these things when it is established in our lives:

> But if I cast out demons by the Spirit of God, then the kingdom of God has come upon you.
>
> —MATTHEW 12:28

The kingdom of God is the rule of God in the spirit realm over the kingdom of darkness ruled by Satan. It is God's authority released through His people that establishes His kingdom in the earth. As we discussed, God's goal is to establish His kingdom on earth as it is in heaven (Matt. 6:10). It was never the plan of God to establish religion; His desire is for relationship. All over the world man has established forms of religion in his pursuit of God. These pursuits are empty if they do not bring His kingdom of righteousness, peace, and joy to earth (Rom. 14:17). In too many cases religion has become man's substitute for relationship. Too many Christians in the church today lack provision because, although they know the King, they do not know about His kingdom. Our provision for the abundant life is found in the kingdom of God:

> But seek first His kingdom and His righteousness, and all these things will be added to you.
>
> —MATTHEW 6:33

God has made provision for His children that comes with entrance into His kingdom; it is part of our divine inheritance that He wants us to have:

> Also we have *obtained* an inheritance, having been predestined according to His purpose...
> —EPHESIANS 1:11, EMPHASIS ADDED

As sons and daughters of God, we are to rule the earth once again. He did not make us slaves who serve the King; we are sons and daughters who rule with the King. As members of the body of Christ in the earth, we can inherit the earth:

> Blessed are the gentle, for they shall inherit the earth.
> —MATTHEW 5:5

God did not create the earth for the devil and his crew. He created it for His children. Through redemption God occupies His children in order to take back the dominion He intended for His children to enjoy.

Establishing the Kingdom of Heaven

The kingdom of heaven is established in the earth when, as believers, we move in authority to bring His kingdom on earth. It is our exercise of dominion on earth that establishes the kingdom of heaven as God rules in righteousness through us. He loves His children and gives us free will to choose relationship with Him. He will not move against our will. It is through our restored relationship that God rules through us in righteousness.

Through the power of the new covenant in the blood of Jesus, the kingdom of heaven came to earth. When a man or woman submits to God, the kingdom of heaven is manifest through them. God indwells believers, giving us His authority to establish His kingdom in the earth.

When that happens, we have the power to bind and loose the will of God into our lives on earth, as we discussed. Matthew 18:18 from the Amplified Bible gives greater clarity for how we bring the kingdom of God to earth:

> Truly I tell you, whatever you forbid and declare to be improper and unlawful on earth must be what is already forbidden in heaven, and whatever you permit and declare proper and lawful on earth must be what is already permitted in heaven.

The key to understanding this verse is that God has a kingdom inventory of provision available in heaven. As we draw on that heavenly inventory of life and blessings, we release His will from heaven into the earth. When we understand His will, we can loose on earth what is already loosed in heaven and forbid on earth what is forbidden in heaven. In other words, we use the authority He gives us for His will to be done in earth as it is in heaven. This is true because we have been given authority over the earth. And God has promised that "He is a rewarder of those who seek Him" (Heb. 11:6). We must first seek Him on earth; then He rewards. This is how we draw on our inheritance.

God could have said, "Behold, I have all authority and you will do what I tell you." This would be a dictator's approach. But God is not a dictator; He is a God of love. If it was up to God to fulfill His program down here, I guarantee you it would have been done by now. But it is not; it is our responsibility to bring the kingdom of heaven to earth. That was God's plan from the beginning—for Adam to live in relationship with God to bring His kingdom to earth. Christ has restored our relationship with God so that we can fulfill the will of God that Adam failed to do. As believers, we are the kingdom of God on the earth. The psalmist understood God's purpose on earth for man:

The highest heavens belong to the LORD, but the earth he has given to man.

—PSALM 115:16, NIV

God gave mankind the earth for two reasons—relationship and rulership. I encounter Christians who do not understand the kingdom Jesus was talking about. There is a tendency among Christians to focus on the *work* of the kingdom rather than the kingdom itself. We want to see the sick healed and we want to walk in health, but we do not bring the kingdom authority to bear that provides those things. Unless our minds are renewed to the kingdom truth, we will not believe in it. The provision of healing and health comes from the kingdom of heaven just as our daily bread does. Remember, Jesus taught us to seek first the kingdom in order for the provisions for life to be added to us. These provisions do not come from the world or from our work; they come from the kingdom of God.

It is the enemy who does not want us to understand the kingdom of God as our source for everything God has provided for life. As the kingdom of God dwells in us through His Spirit, He provides creative power to destroy the work of the enemy as well as natural provision of food and clothing. So the devil tries to get people not to understand this place of provision:

The god of this age has blinded the minds of unbelievers, so that they cannot see the light of the gospel of the glory of Christ, who is the image of God.

—2 CORINTHIANS 4:4

Many times, the enemy uses a spirit of religion to blind the minds of God's people from seeing the truth of the gospel. An unbeliever is simply one who does not believe the truth of God. I do not think this scripture just refers to those who have not accepted Christ as Savior; I think it also refers to the "unbelieving believer." As Christians, if we do not grasp the significance of the kingdom of heaven, we live in a form of religion that denies the power of God. We pray "religious" prayers, and when nothing happens, we blame God. Or worse, some say, "Well, it must be His will for me to be sick! God must have allowed it." What God actually allows is for you and me to have free will with which to choose to bring His kingdom on earth to set the captives free.

Dominion Mandate

The reason God has given us authority is because of our dominion mandate to rule over the earth. God's divine authority gives us the power to enforce that mandate. The kingdom of heaven arrives on earth through enforcement of that authority. The fullness of authority comes by understanding the mandate. If we do not believe we are to rule the earth, we will not exercise our authority in the earth. A policeman is given authority to exhibit power because of the mandate given by the city to keep peace. Similarly, a believer has a spiritual mandate from God to rule the earth by exhibiting authority and power to bring peace through the kingdom of God. In spite of Adam's fall, the mandate found in the first chapter of Genesis has never changed:

> Let Us make man in Our image, according to Our likeness; and let them *rule* over the fish of the sea and over the birds of the sky and over the cattle and over *all the earth*...
> —GENESIS 1:26, EMPHASIS ADDED

When Adam fell, he lost his dominion over the earth. Jesus came to restore that mandate of having dominion over the earth. Now, as a believer, you have authority to enforce the laws of the King in the earth. You cannot do this with a "Rapture mentality," focusing your attention on Christ's return and simply waiting to escape this life. You will have a hard time bringing the kingdom of heaven to earth if you believe you are a part of the failing church, waiting to be bailed out of a world where the enemy is defeating it.

In order to enforce the laws of God in the earth, you have to cultivate a "harvest theology," giving your life to be a part of God's great end-time harvest of souls before Christ's return. Jesus said, "Behold, I have given you authority to tread upon serpents and scorpions, and over all the power of the enemy, and nothing will injure you" (Luke 10:19). As an ambassador of Christ, you have a divine mandate to destroy the works of the enemy in the earth. And Jesus taught that enforcement was required in order to establish His kingdom in the earth:

> From the days of John the Baptist until now the kingdom of heaven suffers violence, and violent men take it by force.
> —MATTHEW 11:12

To take the kingdom by force means to use the power of God to overcome the power of the evil one. That authority, as we discussed, is given to us by Christ to enforce His kingdom law on earth. When the policeman encounters the thief and there is resistance, he uses power to subdue him. A policeman without a mandate does not have the authority to enforce the law. In that same way, a believer must understand his or her mandate in order to move in the authority given them to enforce kingdom law in lawless situations. Where does a policeman get his power? He has a gun and other weapons. Where does a believer get his power? He has God, who gives us His armor to subdue all the enemy's resistance.

Ambassadors

It is important that we understand whom we are to represent in the earth. Jesus came to bring the kingdom of God to you and me to connect us to our assignment to bring the will of our heavenly Father to the earth. To His disciples, Jesus declared that He had conferred a kingdom to them:

> And I confer on you a kingdom, just as my Father conferred one on me.
>
> —LUKE 22:29, NIV

As disciples of Christ, this promise also applies to us, His church in the earth. The apostle James made this very clear when he declared, "Listen, my beloved brethren: did not God choose the poor of this world to be rich in faith and *heirs of the kingdom* which He promised to those who love Him?" (James 2:5, emphasis added). As Jesus continually declared that He was bringing the kingdom of heaven to earth, He was equally clear regarding His mandate for His followers to establish His kingdom in the earth:

> As you go, preach this message: "The kingdom of heaven is near."
>
> —MATTHEW 10:7, NIV

> And he sent them out to preach the kingdom of God and to heal the sick.
>
> —LUKE 9:2, NIV

And the apostle Paul declared that we are ambassadors of God's kingdom:

> Therefore, we are ambassadors for Christ, as though God were making an appeal through us; we beg you on behalf of Christ, be reconciled to God.
>
> —2 CORINTHIANS 5:20

The kingdom of heaven we represent is the kingdom that fulfills the will of God for our own lives. We are privileged to be ambassadors of that heavenly kingdom. Yet we cannot be ambassadors until the King anoints us as His representatives. As Christ represents the Father, we are to represent Him in the earth. As redeemed Christians, we are not just to live in the kingdom of God, pursuing our own goals and waiting for the Rapture to take us to heaven. We are to bring the kingdom of heaven to earth as it is in heaven; that is our assignment as ambassadors of Christ.

The apostle Paul begs believers to be reconciled to God. You cannot represent a kingdom to which you are not reconciled. The Greek word translated as *reconciled* means "to return to favor with, to be received into favor."[4] That requires a change of our mind involving repentance and renewal of our thinking to embrace God's will. In this passage Paul declares that as a believer, you are a new creation, for whom old things are passed away and new things have come (v. 17). Those new things involve your life in the kingdom of God. We now represent, as ambassadors of Christ, another kingdom. Remember, the natural man cannot understand the things of the Spirit; they are spiritually discerned (1 Cor. 2:14). Only by revelation of the Holy Spirit can we understand the kingdom of God.

As Creator, God owns the earth. And after Jesus's resurrection and ascension, He was seated at the right hand of the Father as King over all the earth. And He has given believers authority as ambassadors to establish the kingdom of heaven on earth. Ambassadors represent the kingdom to which they belong, and all their provision comes from the government they represent. Earthly ambassadors have diplomatic immunity, meaning they are not subject to the laws of the kingdom to which they are sent; they are subject only to the laws of the kingdom to which they belong.

Similarly, the Scriptures teach that we are set free from the law of sin and death and now live by the King's law for the kingdom of God to which we belong. Jesus demonstrated this reality to us when He fed five thousand people with only five loaves of bread and two fish.

If His source of provision was from this earthly kingdom, He would have instructed His disciples something like, "This is not enough. Go and buy out the market." But Jesus knew He was an ambassador from another realm; He held the five loaves and two fish up to the God of that supernatural realm, and through supernatural multiplication, there was more than enough food for everyone.

We only lack provision for life when we do not understand our true source for that provision. It is not just saying we belong to the kingdom of God, but it is demonstrating that through faith: "For the kingdom of God does not consist in words but in power" (1 Cor. 4:20). Words alone do not bring the kingdom reality to our lives; a demonstration of power does. It was a demonstration of power that multiplied the loaves and fish. We must express faith in our words, believing the laws of the kingdom to which we belong. We have to change our confession from words that say "this will not work" to words that are faith driven by the will of God.

Unbelief will cause us to say, "Well, that was Jesus. I cannot do that." That is exactly what the devil wants us to believe. Unbelief causes us to line up with the enemy's will; faith causes us to line up with God's will. The kingdom truth is this: "*You* will receive power when the Holy Spirit has come upon you" (Acts 1:8, emphasis added). You and I receive power to demonstrate the kingdom of God in our lives on the earth. For that to be a reality, we must continually choose to partner with the Holy Spirit to be the vessels of His power.

Our Divine "Immune System"

As ambassadors, we are Christ's diplomats to the nations; we represent the King and His kingdom of righteousness and love. As I mentioned, this is possible because our King has set us free from the law of sin and death:

> For the law of the Spirit of life in Christ Jesus has set you free from the law of sin and of death.
>
> —ROMANS 8:2

Through our divine "immune system" we are no longer subject to the law of sin from which we have been set free. We now live by the law of the Spirit of life in Christ Jesus. As ambassadors or diplomats of the kingdom of God, we have "diplomatic immunity" from the law of sin and death perpetrated on earth by the kingdom of darkness. The purpose for which we are redeemed is "so that we would receive the promise of the Spirit through faith" (Gal. 3:14). We cannot receive the promise if we are living with the curse in unbelief.

Is sickness part of the curse from which we have been redeemed? God has set up a kingdom "immune system" for us to live free from sickness. The question we must ask ourselves is: Are we living in it? If not, how do we learn to live in that freedom Christ offers? We live in it by the promise of the Spirit through our faith.

Christ rescued you; He bought you back through redemption. Jesus paid for your sin (and sickness) through His sacrifice on Calvary. He paid for it so that you would not have to. The devil brings sickness to steal that redemption from you. Your immunity from his destructions means you don't have to live there any longer. In Christ, you have been made complete, whole, and free from any of the enemy's power.

> For in Him all the fullness of Deity dwells in bodily form, and in Him you have been made complete, and He is the head over all rule and authority.
>
> —COLOSSIANS 2:9–10

If we have been made complete, why should we not be able to live completely free from sin and sickness? The capacity that we have as believers is to have the fullness of the Deity dwelling within us, to be complete in Him. His divine presence does not just affect the spirit of mankind; it is also meant to affect our soul and body. As born-again believers, we are the temple of the Holy Spirit, who dwells in us. Why should the body of Christ not achieve all that redemption has provided? Jesus is the head of His body in the earth; He sits at the right hand of the Father giving us access to all the provision of His divine kingdom. *The body of Christ will not achieve fullness of redemption until we believe this kingdom reality.*

As ambassadors of the kingdom of God to which we have been reconciled, we have access to the fullness of the Father, the fullness of the Son, and the fullness of the Holy Spirit. God does not see us condemned to live under the curse of sin; He only sees us as the righteousness of God through the blood of Christ. When we begin, by faith, to see ourselves as He sees us, sickness will no longer violate our "immune system."

Jesus declared that He had glorified the Father through His work on the earth (John 17:4). As members of the body of Christ, we are to bring glory to the Father. The greatest glory we can give the Father is when we walk complete in Him, receiving the divine health that He provided. The Father's will was to send His Son to redeem us back to a sinless position, a place where sin and sickness no longer have power to rule in our lives.

Where Is the Kingdom?

During my first twenty-five years of serving God in the church, if you asked me, "Where is the kingdom of God?", I would answer, "It is where God is in heaven." While this is partly true, my limited understanding was that heaven was the only place where the kingdom of God exists. I thought that if I was ever to experience the kingdom reality, Jesus would have to return and take me to heaven (the Rapture) so I could see it.

To me the kingdom was not near me; it was faraway. I was not able to walk in authority because, in my thinking, that belonged to a future kingdom. My unrenewed mind said, "Well, it is all up to God; if He wants something to happen here, He will do it." So I could not figure out why nothing was happening. Then I would think, "Well, I guess God has His reasons."

After the Holy Spirit began to reveal the kingdom of God to me, He showed me that the kingdom I thought only existed in the future in heaven was available today on the earth. It was this kingdom that Jesus taught when He was here, promising that He would give me the authority to become victorious in life.

When Jesus said the kingdom "is come upon you" (Matt. 12:28), He meant it was not far away; it is at hand, near to where we are. Jesus was establishing His kingdom, His foundation of power, in the lives of His followers when He declared, "Behold, I have given you authority to tread on serpents and scorpions, and over all the power of the enemy" (Luke 10:19). We are given the status of royalty in the kingdom of God, with power to reign as ambassadors of that kingdom. As ambassadors of the King, we are also called a royal priesthood:

> But you are a chosen race, a royal priesthood, a holy nation, a people for God's own possession, so that you may proclaim the excellencies of Him who has called you out of darkness into His marvelous light.
>
> —1 PETER 2:9

As born-again Christians, we are God's possession. He possesses us with His Spirit. It is by His possession of us that we have power to proclaim the truth of His kingdom. We understand the mysteries of the kingdom of God (Matt. 13:11) and demonstrate its reality in our lives:

> For the kingdom of God is not eating and drinking, but righteousness and peace and joy in the Holy Spirit.
>
> —ROMANS 14:17

The kingdom of God does not consist of natural things but of supernatural. It is reflected in life in the Holy Spirit, which is "righteousness and peace and joy." As the righteousness of God in Christ (2 Cor. 5:21), believers are reconciled to the kingdom of God; we are in right standing with Him and have authority to reign with Him. Jesus gave us His peace and told us not to be troubled (John 14:27) but to focus on His victory in overcoming the world. And He gave us His joy, "that your joy may be made full" (John 15:11). In this kingdom reality of righteousness, peace, and joy, the believer dwells in victory; it is a result of relationship with the Holy Spirit. Jesus described this relationship when He told us where to look for the kingdom of God:

> The kingdom of God does not come with observation; nor will they say, "See here!" or, "See there!" For indeed, the kingdom of God is within you.
>
> —LUKE 17:20–21, NKJV

Jesus declared that the kingdom of God is within the believer. Because the kingdom of God is in the Holy Spirit and the Holy Spirit is in us, we have the kingdom within us. The kingdom is not in the natural "observing" realm; it is in the supernatural realm of the Spirit of God within the believer. The kingdom of God is established in what we do not see, the spirit realm; its effects are experienced in the redemption of what we do see, the natural realm. If there is ever a reason to partner with the Holy Spirit, this is it.

Understanding Authority

Greater understanding of the divine authority that has been given to us will help us to live victorious lives in Christ. As we have discussed, the kingdom of God is the authority of God within the heart and spirit of man. As we exercise that authority, we fulfill the will of God for our lives and bring the kingdom of God to earth:

> Thy kingdom come. Thy will be done in earth, as it is in heaven.
> —MATTHEW 6:10, KJV

Jesus taught us to pray, "Thy kingdom come." That happens when the Holy Spirit takes up residence within your spirit through redemption. Jesus continued, "Thy will be done on earth...." His kingdom must come so that His will can be done on earth as it is in heaven. The authority to fulfill the will of God comes by the Spirit of God dwelling within us. Amazingly, the will of God is done on the earth through men and women to whom God has given authority. We have authority because the Spirit of God, who is all authority, dwells in us. When we understand this divine reality, we can move in His fullness of authority. The power to exhibit authority comes by the Holy Spirit. The apostle Paul understood the power of the kingdom of God within the believer when he prayed:

> I pray that the eyes of your heart may be enlightened, so that you will know what is the hope of His calling, what are the riches of the glory of His inheritance in the saints.
> —EPHESIANS 1:18

God is saying He has an *inheritance* in His saints by means of His acquisition, His possession of us through redemption. The Scriptures teach, as we have discussed, that we were bought with a price; God purchased His people and gave them an inheritance. There are true *riches* in His inheritance, that is, abundance and wealth. The apostle

Paul is praying that our eyes will be open to this revelation so that we will know what is the hope of God's kingdom calling:

> And what is the surpassing greatness of His power toward us who believe. These are in accordance with the working of the strength of His might which He brought about in Christ, when He raised Him from the dead and seated Him at His right hand in the heavenly places.
>
> —EPHESIANS 1:19–20

A proper understanding of the power and authority we have in Christ involves our knowing that it comes by God and not by us. Having this revelation will bring us to the wonderful fulfillment of the promise: "Now to Him who is able to do far more abundantly beyond all that we ask or think, according to the power that works within us" (Eph. 3:20).

When we are filled or possessed by God, we can become conformed to His image. He can release His supernatural power through us, which gives us authority to fulfill His will on the earth. The way to overcome our enemy is to be overcome by our God.

God has given His church divine authority to make known the mysteries of God's kingdom to the rulers of this world and of heavenly places:

> …and to bring to light what is the administration of the mystery which for ages has been hidden in God who created all things; so that the manifold wisdom of God might now be made known through the church to the rulers and the authorities in the heavenly places.
>
> —EPHESIANS 3:9–10

The church, the body of Christ in the earth, is to make known the things of the kingdom of heaven to the rulers of this world. As believers we are kingdom warriors, clothed with the armor of God;

we are bred to fight. We are to destroy the work of the enemy and take back what he has stolen. Too many Christians fear the enemy because they do not understand the authority within them. God has the only army that shows up on the battlefield not expecting anyone to be there. Victory is certain through the authority of God that dwells in us. The devil is not an issue to God. God is the Creator. The devil is a created, fallen being; he has never created anything.

Traffic Cop

The enemy will measure a believer by how that believer sees himself or herself. If we do not see ourselves with authority over our enemy, then we will believe the enemy has authority over us. Instead of believing the truth, we believe the lie of the enemy. What we believe determines what we receive. Let me illustrate.

If you went down to a busy intersection where there was a street light and started directing traffic dressed as you are, what would happen to you? You might just get run over, honked at, or yelled at because no one recognizes your authority to direct traffic. But if you were hired by the police department and you put on the uniform of a policeman, you could step into that intersection and expect people to stop and go at your command. Why? Because they recognize the authority given to you by the uniform you wear. You would not have any more power than you had in your street clothes. But because you have authority that is readily recognized, you have power to make them stop. Your authority comes from whom you represent: law enforcement empowered by the city. When it is recognized, it gives you the power to direct traffic. Authority is exercised through recognition; your power is not in yourself but in the authority you represent.

As believers who have the kingdom of God indwelling us, we have authority given to us by God. Yet if we fail to "put on the full armor of God" (Eph. 6:13, NIV), our authority will go unrecognized. We will become vulnerable to the destructions of the evil one. Our power to live victoriously in Christ comes from who we are in Him. In our own strength we will only struggle; in the strength of God we overcome.

Faith or Doubt?

Kingdom authority should cause us to move in a confidence that vanquishes doubt. Doubt is the doorway the enemy uses to gain access to our authority. Faith exercises authority; doubt hinders it. Jesus taught us the difference between the power of faith and the problem of doubt:

> Truly I say to you, if you have faith, and do not doubt, you will not only do what was done to the fig tree, but even if you say to this mountain, "Be taken up and cast into the sea," it will happen. And all things you ask in prayer, believing, you shall receive.
> —MATTHEW 21:21–22

The Greek word translated "doubt" means "to separate, to withdraw from or oppose."[5] Doubt comes to oppose the Word of God that produces faith. Doubt comes from the enemy to separate a believer from God. It is in direct opposition to our faith, and its intent is to cut off our ability to receive. When the enemy causes us to doubt that we are healed, doubt opposes our faith that says we are. If we doubt we are healed, according to the Word we cannot receive our healing.

Faith requires us to believe God; doubt does not. What gives the traffic cop courage to stand in that busy intersection is believing he has authority. The response he gets from the traffic comes out of his belief system. If he doubted that he had authority to direct traffic as a uniformed policeman, he would never step into the intersection. When we have faith to believe, all things are possible. God uses faith that we exercise to establish His will on the earth. The enemy uses doubt to cut it off.

Doubt Brings Failure

Do you believe you can walk in health, or do you doubt that you can? Too many believers are living with failure rather embracing truth by faith, which brings success. God cannot fail. Only man can fail by living outside of God's realm. The very purpose of the kingdom of heaven arriving on earth is to overcome failure. As believers, when we embrace the kingdom that is within us; we possess God's grace (ability) to turn failure into success. Failure should always provide a target for the kingdom of God within us to overcome. Failure cannot exist unless we give up on God, for with God all things are possible (Luke 1:37).

Failure says: "This situation is impossible." "That good thing cannot happen." "It just will not work." "It is too late." Past failure will sometimes set up doubt, preventing your faith from being exercised, and keep the kingdom of God from coming into your situation. That is why it is important to be filled with the Word of God, which produces faith so that failure can be overcome.

The disciples were filled with doubt on one occasion about the possibility of anyone being saved. But Jesus said to them, "With men this is impossible, but with God all things are possible" (Matt. 19:26, NKJV). Jesus was saying in essence, that when things appear impossible, it is time for God to intervene. We will believe things are impossible when we focus on our own power or lack of it, our own failure, which is simply a lack of success. Our failure brings fear to our hearts, and fear cuts off faith, which prevents the "all things are possible" for God.

If all things are possible for God and He dwells within us, how can we fail? Jesus also explained that, if we give good things to our children, "how much more will your Father who is in heaven give good things to those who ask Him!" (Matt. 7:11). The will of God for us is always good. It is never His will that we suffer failure. Failure will never fulfill the will of God. Instead, God promises that we should fulfill His good works:

> For we are His workmanship, created in Christ Jesus for good works, which God prepared beforehand so that we would walk in them.
>
> —EPHESIANS 2:10

We are not made for failure; we are created for good works. God prepared those good works beforehand for those who dare to become "His workmanship" in the earth. The apostle John confirmed our mandate to do "good" as believers:

> Beloved, do not imitate what is evil, but what is good. The one who does good is of God; the one who does evil has not seen God.
>
> —3 JOHN 11

We are told not to imitate what is evil; anything that is hurtful and does harm can be considered to be evil. Failure does all of these things. The kingdom of God will always produce success.

When I began my journey to health, I started with the Holy Spirit, who guarantees our success. I understood that I am His workmanship prepared for success beforehand so that I can walk in it. God's will always moves me toward success. In this process of regaining my health, I knew that failure could not exist as long as I embraced what God was doing.

Failure is man's measurement determined outside of God's will. Failure can only be established in our "impossible" situations when we give up on God. A Christian cannot fail when he or she moves in Christ, because with Christ all things are possible. Faith moves the possible realm of God's kingdom into our impossible realm. Prevailing faith becomes creative as it moves substance into what we hope for. Through this divine process we overcome failure.

When change, spiritual growth, no longer exists in our lives, we are set up for failure. When the kingdom is no longer expanding in our lives, we are at risk of failure. It is kingdom authority that provides the power to move out of failure. Failure is always guaranteed when we quit believing the Word of God. As Christians, we cannot fail as long as we move in Christ's truth.

Failure requires a decision backed up by no effort. It does not take power to fail; a lack of effort will result in failure. Success requires plans and actions, without which you will suffer poverty in every area of life. Time alone will bring poverty, because living in poverty requires nothing of you. God has a plan that requires action. When you act upon His kingdom plan, He provides your success to overcome poverty and failure. You suffer failure when you do not achieve your goal; you always experience success when you achieve His goal.

Too many cannot see their future because they are measuring it by their past failures. The enemy uses failure to steal your future. Your past is called "past" because it is over. If you want to move in God's power, you will have to move out of failure. To success, failure is simply something to overcome. Kingdom authority comes when you submit to the power of the Holy Spirit, who will establish your future.

You do not have to take what the enemy has planned for you unless you are defeated. Failure results in defeat, allowing the enemy to pilfer from you. In war, when the enemy is defeated, the victor moves in to take the spoils. Why should you admit defeat when you overwhelmingly conquer by the power of God? You can only be defeated when you believe the lies of an enemy who, in reality, does not have the power to win. Failure only comes when you give up and admit defeat.

Kingdom Success

Your success or failure is not determined by your circumstances. In the world, wealth is success. In the kingdom, success is wealth. When you come to the revelation of who God is within, you will become successful because you now do all things through Christ. Success is positional; failure is conditional.

Your position of success will change your condition of failure. When you walk in the Holy Spirit, you walk in the fullness of the kingdom of God that is greater than anything of this world.

> How blessed is the man who does not walk in the council of the wicked, nor stand in the path of sinners, nor sit in the seat of scoffers! But his delight is in the law of the LORD, and in His law he meditates day and night. He will be like a tree firmly planted by streams of water, which yields its fruit in its season and its leaf does not wither; and in whatever he does, he prospers.
>
> —PSALM 1:1–3

Blessing comes when we walk in the light of God's Word. Failure comes when we walk according to the world's order of things. The Scriptures teach that we are in the world but not of the world. We are exhorted not to take counsel from a fallen world (Rom. 12:2). We are not to set our minds on the things of earth but on the things above where God is (Col. 3:2). Why do we believe we can have success when we take counsel from a world steeped in failure?

We are blessed when we delight in the truth of God. The psalmist declared that when we meditate on God's truth day and night, it will cause us to be like a tree firmly rooted in kingdom authority. It will cause us to prosper in the will of God. A full-time God gives us a full-time result of blessing. When the will of God is fulfilled in our lives, we become successful because truth sets us free to walk in the Spirit:

> …so that the requirement of the Law might be fulfilled in us, who do not walk according to the flesh but according to the Spirit.
>
> —ROMANS 8:4

This Christian life is a kingdom partnership; when we walk according to the Spirit, the authority and the power of the Spirit fulfills the will of God in our lives. In the kingdom of God the will of God has the true DNA of man in it. It was designed for us. As seed it comes fulfilled.

It is clear from the Scriptures that God wants His children to prosper in all of life, including walking in health (3 John 2). God never meant for you to have to earn your prosperity in Him; it has been willed to you. Your redemption was purchased by Jesus on your behalf. You have a right to possess the blessing of health because it already belongs to you. Prosperity in God is not the world's idea of wealth. Prosperity and health are given according to God's will for every one of His children.

God takes pleasure in your prosperity, as the psalmist declared: "The LORD be magnified, who delights in the prosperity of His servant" (Ps. 35:27). The word *prosperity* is translated from the Hebrew *shalowm*, which means "welfare, health, prosperity, peace and contentment."[6] In Christ you have been made complete (Col. 2:10) so that as a possession of God you can enjoy the prosperity of God. The Holy Spirit was given to you "as a pledge of our inheritance, with a view to the redemption of God's own possession" (Eph. 1:14). His will supplies you with all you need to live in wholeness:

> And God is able to make *all* grace abound to you, so that always having *all* sufficiency in everything, you may have an abundance for every good deed.
> —2 CORINTHIANS 9:8, EMPHASIS ADDED

When you partner with the Spirit of God, He is able to release His grace to you so that you will have all sufficiency in everything. It does not say *some* sufficiency in *some* things. *All* sufficiency in everything is an abundance for every good thing you are called to do. How could you not be successful when God gives you all sufficiency in everything? How can you be lacking when you have an abundance for every good work?

As believers, we must strive to walk in this abundance. We must cry out, "Holy Spirit, come!" We must embrace the Holy Spirit as the source of our very lives. We must hear what He is saying to us and then obey what He wants to do. Our very lives must become His life. Our desire must be His desire. His desire is that we be blessed with an abundance for everything He calls us to accomplish in the kingdom of God.

We must not allow the enemy to use the circumstances of the world to defeat us. Our success is not determined by what we possess on earth; it is determined by what we possess in the kingdom of heaven. Our prosperity is not determined by what we get but by who we are. The Word of God teaches that we are the righteousness of Christ; we are mighty in God; we are more than conquerors; we are a royal priesthood.

Breakthrough

In summary, what we have been discussing is how to achieve breakthrough into the power and authority of the kingdom of God. For years I have heard people in the church talking about our need to have breakthrough. We fast for breakthrough; we are praying for God's people to have breakthrough; pastors are preaching about the need for breakthrough. I remember talking about the need for breakthrough after I first got saved. Years later we are still trying to get breakthrough.

According to Webster's Dictionary, *breakthrough* is defined as "an offensive thrust that penetrates and carries beyond a defensive line in warfare; a sudden advance."[7] A spiritual breakthrough does happen where we are; it takes us where we need to be. We cannot have breakthrough until we break *out*! We must break out from the mentality of failure and captivity where we have been living and break into the freedom where God is calling us to walk. We have to break out of wrong mind-sets. We have to break out of our tradition that prevents change. We have to break out of religious teachings that have bound us up. We have to break out of the influence of the world. We have to break out of walking by sight instead of walking in faith.

When we break out of these bondages, we can move past them into the liberty we have in Christ. These are strongholds of the enemy that prevent us from having breakthrough. When the stronghold is broken, we move through it into liberty. It is the enemy's defense that creates a stronghold to prevent us from breaking through to access the power of God we have been given. The enemy wants to put us in a "concentration camp," a place where we are fenced in and can only concentrate on him. He knows if we can break out, we will only concentrate on God.

It is that supernatural breakout that brings the advance to move beyond the enemy's defense into kingdom living. We break out of limitation and into a full-time God. We break out of deception into the revelation of the Holy Spirit. We break out of lies into a truth that sets us free. We break out of weakness into the fullness of authority. We break out of thoughts of defeat into a mind that is renewed to heaven's possibilities. We break out of the natural into the supernatural where we can experience all the possibilities of God. When our breakout brings the breakthrough, we will experience the full potential of being a "new creation." Old things will fall away; all things will become new and these new things will be of God.

Chapter 7

YOUR PERSONAL HEALTH CARE SYSTEM

Healing is the process for establishing health.

My goal in this chapter is to encourage you to begin the process of establishing your personal health care program. There are numerous valid nutritional and exercise programs available for you to utilize in your process of establishing your health. It is up to you to search out which program will work for your body and your personal circumstances. I am not suggesting a particular nutritional or exercise program for you to use. Rather, I want you to understand why it is necessary to establish good nutrition and exercise for your overall health.

You Are What You Eat

How do we get in such bad shape? Why do we gain unwanted weight and become weak and unhealthy? The answer can be expressed in the adage "You are what you eat." Most of my life I thought I could go to the grocery store and buy anything that was on the shelf and eat it. After all, I thought, no one would be allowed to have products marketed there that would hurt me. So Michelle and I bought these packaged foods, took them home, prepared meals, and ate them.

As the years went by, we noticed we were gaining weight. The older we got, the fatter we got. The fatter we got, the weaker we became. We thought gaining weight with age was normal because everyone around us was having the same problem.

As I mentioned, there was always an answer for our weight problem advertised on TV. There were diet programs and exercise devices that were marketed for the masses. From time to time we would try a diet or buy one of these devices we saw advertised. We did not change our eating habits but kept eating the processed foods we bought.

Surprisingly, the diets did not work. We accumulated a variety of exercise devices, which we stored in our basement. I noticed we were not the only ones experiencing a weight problem. From reports in the media, it seemed the whole country was having a weight problem. To help us with our overweight problem, we started buying packaged foods that were labeled "fat free." I thought, "Well, this makes sense. I am having a fat problem, so maybe fat-free foods will solve it." But sadly, eating fat-free foods did not solve my fat problem. When we would gather with our friends and discuss openly our weight problem, we just concluded that it must be because of age. That justification made me feel better for a while.

Then I noticed we were having health issues as well. So, since the diet and exercise solutions did not work, we would try the pill solution. I could still eat the foods that were making me unhealthy and then solve the problem by buying some pills. There seemed to be a pill solution for every food problem. When I turned on the TV, there was another pill or drug advertised for another condition. I did wonder, "Why are they advertising to me? Isn't the doctor supposed to prescribe medicine? I am not the drug expert; the doctor is."

I also noticed that with every drug advertised, they had to state the side effects caused by the drug. Some of those side effects were worse than the problem I was trying to get rid of. Then I began to notice ads from law offices where attorneys wanted to represent people who had suffered the side effects of these wonder drugs. It didn't take rocket science to figure out that something was not working here. After my heart attack, I decided this media blitz was contributing to my wrong thinking about health.

I soon began to discover that I was becoming what I was eating. I began to understand that processed foods are called "processed" for a reason; most of the natural nutritional value of the food has been processed out. In addition, what was added were artificial flavors and additives to make the "artificial" taste better. I learned that these processed foods lacked the vitamins and minerals that my body needed to be healthy. In many cases, some form of sugar or high-fructose corn syrup was added in place of vitamins and minerals. When I ate these packaged foods, I was not satisfied because I was not receiving the nutrition my body needed, so I ate more. The more I ate to try to satisfy my hunger, the more weight I gained. And I did notice that I seemed to be contributing to the success of these "processed foods" companies, along with many others.

Is What You Eat Making You Sick?

Did you know that processed foods are treated with more than six thousand chemical additives to color, stabilize, emulsify, bleach, texturize, soften, sweeten, flavor, hide odors, and preserve the "food" you are putting into your body?[1] Preservatives are added to food to prevent spoiling, and pesticides are sprayed on fruits and vegetables. Growth hormones are added to the feed of the animals we eat, and artificial sweeteners are added to create taste. The problem is when we ingest these toxic chemicals, our body has difficulty metabolizing them. They then begin to build up in our body and cause various diseases.

The problem is that these chemicals are not in just a few foods; they are found in most foods we consume. On the average, the human body can effectively process and expel 1.2 million toxins in twenty-four hours. The problem is we take in over 2 million toxins a day through air pollution, water, food, beverages, prescription drugs, parasites, stress, heavy metals, and radiation from various sources.[2] This toxic overload creates havoc with the body's ability to function effectively. When our food supply does not provide proper nutrition, the situation is compounded because our body's immune system cannot effectively eliminate toxins when it is compromised through lack of nutrition.

Over a period of time, the body's ability to keep up with the onslaught begins to weaken. We gain weight, become tired, lose energy, and no longer have a healthy immune system capable of fighting off sickness. We have to take supplements and prescribed drugs that do not solve the problem but just help to manage it until we die. We call this "health care," but it would be more accurately called "disease management."

I remember one occasion several years ago when I was riding my mountain bike on a sidewalk and noticed that someone had dropped an ice cream cone just ahead. I concluded that someone had just dropped it because it had not yet melted. The next day I rode my bike on that same route, and there was that ice cream cone—it still had not melted. I wonder how much ice cream was in that cone and how much was pure preservative to make it last that long?

Our Sweet Tooth

I did not realize the destructive effect that sugar had on my life. Isn't it interesting how we refer to our consumption of sugar as satisfying our "sweet tooth"? It causes us to have affection or love for something that is not good for us. We become addicted to sweets. I have come to believe that sugar is one of the most addictive substances on the planet.

The average American consumes 2–3 pounds of sugar each week. Refined sugars come in three main forms: sucrose (table sugar), dextrose (corn sugar), and high-fructose corn syrup. These sugars are processed into breads, cereals, ketchup, spaghetti sauce, mayonnaise, peanut butter, premade meals, and desserts. The average American consumes up to 135 pounds of sugar through these sources per year.

The health problems caused by overeating sugary foods result from the impact sugar has on raising insulin levels, inhibiting the release of growth hormones, which depresses the immune system, resulting in disease.[3]

A high influx of sugar into the blood stream will causes an imbalance to the body's blood sugar levels, requiring a release of more insulin, the body's defense mechanism to help keep your blood sugar at safe levels. The increased insulin also promotes the storage of fat, enabling rapid weight gain and elevated triglyceride levels, both of which have been linked to cardiovascular disease.[4] America has one of the most advanced medical industries in the world, yet we are some of the sickest people as well.

An Obese Nation

The very food I thought was safe for me to eat because it was on the shelves of the grocery store was causing obesity and heart disease. The Centers for Disease Control and Prevention (CDC) reported that in 2008 there were 72 million Americans who were considered obese. Of those, 24 million suffered diabetes as a result.[5] In addition, two-thirds of all Americans are overweight. Overweight and obesity put our population at risk for coronary heart disease, hypertension, stroke, type 2 diabetes, certain types of cancer, and premature death.

USA Today reported recently that in 2008, Americans who were thirty or more pounds over a healthy weight cost the country an estimated $147 billion in weight-related medical bills.[6] In 2010, nearly half of all doctor visits were made by the baby boomer generation.[7]

I always thought the word *malnutrition* referred to third-world countries where there was a lack of resources and extreme poverty. I discovered that *mal* simply means "bad." In other words, bad nutrition has made us a malnourished nation. We are a nation of people with bad nutrition, causing weakened immune systems and allowing sickness to invade at will. When we consider walking in health and receiving healing, we have to understand the issue of becoming "stewards" for our bodies to maintain their health.

While we as a nation continue to gain weight, we see the rate of diabetes spiral out of control. This becomes serious when we see children, increasingly overweight and obese, contracting this disease in ever larger numbers. Our health officials have become concerned about how to stop this rise of obesity. Not only does it put a stress upon our health system, but the future cost of treatment is almost impossible to measure. The national news media are now saying that other nations are also seeing an increase of obesity, perhaps from adopting some of our Western eating patterns.

Pandemic

The CDC calls the rise of obesity in America a pandemic.[8] *Pandemic* as used in medicine refers to an epidemic of disease that spreads over a very wide area, such as an entire country or continent. I believe that a pandemic disease or health problem is driven by demonic forces that want God's people to suffer the pangs of pandemonium. The devil's goal to kill, steal, and destroy is aided mightily when he can manage to perpetrate a pandemic of evil by whatever means. He is perpetrating a pandemic of obesity across our nation. And he wants to pull the wool over the eyes of believers so that they do not use the spiritual weapons of their warfare against this destructive obesity pandemic. The enemy wants believers to battle disease through natural means while principalities and demonic forces overpower us. This struggle against malnutrition and obesity is not a battle against "flesh and blood" (Eph. 6:12); it is a spiritual battle against principalities and powers that we have authority to win by the Holy Spirit.

The deception of demonic forces is driving a food industry that has a profit motive. Out of this motivation to cater to the "natural appetites" of people in order to reap great profits comes food that causes addiction and dependency and food products that lack nutrition and depress our immune systems. They produce an obese nation that cannot protect itself from the onslaught of sickness and disease. Collectively, we have become a people who are overweight and out of shape. Rather than to fight against and overcome our food addiction problems, we find ways to accommodate them through support groups, increasing use of drugs, more doctor visits, and various other support apparatuses that we call "health care."

Sadly, the rate of obesity and related health problems worsening in America are also worsening in the church in America. The danger increases for believers who do not think that eating-related illnesses are a spiritual problem. They allow the enemy to invade their body, not realizing that he wants to destroy any person or nation that follows God and that he will use any means he can to accomplish his destructions.

The devil can cause even a wealthy nation to suffer poverty of health as well as financial poverty from overwhelming health care costs. According to Webster's dictionary, *poverty* involves not just a lack of sufficient finances, but also debility due to malnutrition and lack of fertility of the soil.[9]

I am not writing these things to make people with health issues feel guilty. I am only discussing them to point out that these self-inflicted health issues are not the will of God. They are the will of the enemy who wants to destroy as many as possible through an obesity pandemic. We perish for lack of knowledge, but truth sets us free. The very enemy who is the author of sickness is preparing people's minds to accept sickness. He is weakening bodies so that they no longer have resistance to preventable health issues. He knows if he can take this fight out of the hands of God, he can win. He does that by convincing the church that this battle is not a spiritual battle; obesity is simply a part of our culture. The good news is that when we realize the spiritual battle we are in, we can resist the devil and be victorious:

> Submit therefore to God. Resist the devil and he will flee from you.
> —JAMES 4:7

We do not have the power to resist if we have chosen to accommodate a situation. In the case of food consumption and our health, as long as we choose to accommodate our wrong eating habits, we will not be able to resist the destructive plan of the devil against our health. The key is to submit to God in our health concerns and resist the devil's plan. When we submit to God, all things are possible.

Real Food

When I was unhealthy and overweight, I did not know what real food was. My idea of real food was any food that tastes good. Everything I did revolved around food. If I was watching TV at home, I would eat snacks. There were snacks for playing cards, for going to the movies, for taking a long drive. There were vacation snacks, holiday snacks, and pretty much a snack for all occasions. These were all the things that taste good because they were either made up of mostly carbs or sugar. This was the stuff I ate between breakfast, lunch, and dinner.

For meals, as I mentioned, I ate the packaged, processed foods that were easy to prepare. Sometimes we would buy the packaged meal that was labeled "fat free," as I mentioned earlier, to make us feel better about our weight issues. Neither my wife, Michelle, nor I like to cook. Yet we lived to eat. We did not eat to live. I had noticed that, though I was eating all the time, I was also hungry all the time. I simply thought this was the way we were all supposed to eat. I did not realize the toll it was taking on my body.

Looking back, I realize I was too much like the proverbial "frog in the pot." You know, you can put a frog in a pot of cool water on the stove and slowly turn up the heat. The frog will not jump out of the pot as the water gets hotter; it does not recognize the gradual change in temperature until too late, and it gets boiled. The frog feels safe in the water: "I am a frog; I belong in the water." I felt safe eating foods I enjoyed and did not realize what was slowly happening to the health of my body until it was almost too late.

The goal of the enemy is to make us believe that the way we are eating is all right. We do not realize what is happening day by day to our bodies. We are just one in the crowd going where everybody else is going—to our favorite eating places. Association results in assimilation. What we face is what we embrace. We have a hard time recognizing an enemy that has become familiar. The food that I was embracing was killing me. It caused me to be obese, weak, and sick, ending in a life-threatening heart attack, as I shared earlier.

When Mr. Universe came to our house, he began to talk to us about real food and the kinds of food that God intended for us to eat—foods that would fuel our bodies and make them healthy, the kinds of foods that would build up our immune systems. Real foods are whole foods or natural foods that are not altered by processing or refining. Whole foods usually do not contain added ingredients such as sugar, salt, fats, or chemicals that alter or accelerate growth. Fruits and vegetables; unpolished grains; unprocessed meat, poultry, and fish; and nonhomogenized milk are all examples of whole foods. Consuming these nutritious foods in our diet produces many health benefits. Our weight will normalize to what it should be for our age and height.

Consuming a diet of whole foods, along with doing proper exercise, will not only bring your weight down, but also it has been shown to reverse type 2 diabetes. It will boost your immune system to defend against disease. You will have more energy as your body receives the fuel it needs. As your body becomes healthy, you will develop a sense of well-being in body, mind, and spirit. A sense of well-being comes from being well. When your physical body becomes well, it reflects light and life upon your spirit man. Conversely, when you are sick, the physical man becomes a drag upon the spirit man. It is difficult to renew your mind with the truth of God when you are hampered both physically and spiritually by poor eating habits. God provides nutritional foods that keep your triune person healthy.

So where do you find real foods? My goal here is to heighten your awareness of healthy and unhealthy food choices. It is up to each one of you to begin to go down the road of discovery for your own good. There are resources everywhere that give information on whole foods or natural foods, telling where to buy them and how to prepare them. There are health food stores, farmer's markets, and organic markets and grocery stores. You can learn from books, CDs, wellness seminars, friends, nutritionists, and online health information sites.

When I first began to change my diet, I thought that whole or organic foods were going to be too costly for us to purchase. But when I added up the medical costs of doctor visits, prescription drugs, hospital costs, and the cost of lost time given to managing my unhealthy body, I soon learned the cost for proper nutrition to have a healthy body was not so bad. I soon began to enjoy the health benefits that Michelle and I received from eating a good diet and exercising. We felt better and had the energy to go out and enjoy ourselves. We worked together on our meal plans. We would go to the farmer's market for fresh fruits and vegetables. We found great meal recipes that we both liked. And we supported each other with encouragement when we needed it.

Every Body Is Different

It is important to realize that we are all different. Each person thinks differently and eats differently. God made each of our bodies, yet we all have different physical needs and preferences. We must realize that we cannot embrace what one person does as right and try to force it on another person. But the general principle we must follow is to eat right and exercise.

In our journey to health, I discovered early on that the whole foods I eat, Michelle may not eat. Her body is different from mine; she has different needs and preferences. How I exercise is different from how she exercise. I might use weights while she uses the treadmill or aerobic DVDs. Our different approaches to health do not mean we cannot work together toward the same goal. It does mean we do not try to force what we do on each other.

We share our successes and edify one another through encouragement. Our overriding desire is to live together "long and strong." We have decided that our age will not determine our health. It will be the lifestyle choices we make together that will determine our health. In this way we know we will be faithful to God and to one another. We have embraced this proverb: "But a faithful ambassador brings health" (Prov. 13:17, NKJV). We are ambassadors of God, who desire our health; therefore we are committed to bring His kingdom of health to the earth.

Stressed Out

It does not do you any good to get your diet in good order, begin an exercise program, and then get stressed out about it. As a matter of fact, stress can sideline the whole process for pursuing health. Becoming healthy should not be stressful; worrying about it can be. You may be aware that your body responds to stress by releasing stress hormones. These hormones help you to deal with "fight-or-flight" situations that require strength or speed.

Stress hormones increase blood pressure, heart rate, and blood sugar levels to give you the quick response needed to respond to danger. However, chronic stress due to worry, fear, or other problems can become harmful to your health. Chronic stress can weaken your immune system and increase the risk of obesity, heart disease, depression, and various other illnesses. Chronic stress can also prevent your body's fat-burning mechanism. You may be eating and working out but not losing weight because of stress. Many adults suffer adverse health effects from stress. Up to 90 percent of doctor visits are estimated to be at least partially for stress-related symptoms and complaints.[10]

You need to understand that your personal health care program is a *lifestyle*, not a destination. You may start out terribly overweight and out of shape. You might think, "How can I do this at my age?" Your mountain of health issues might seem insurmountable. But remember: with God all things are possible. You will become stressed and want to quit if you focus on the mountain; you can make it disappear when you focus on God. When you have the peace of God, you will also have the strength of God to overcome.

> These things I have spoken to you, so that in Me you may have peace. In the world you have tribulation, but take courage; I have overcome the world.
>
> —JOHN 16:33

The *peace* Jesus promised to His followers involves harmony, security, safety, prosperity and happiness.[11] It is a picture of success in life in spite of the trouble in the world. The Lord is saying that in Him you will have success in all you do because you are joined to Him. The tribulation of the world, the things you have to overcome, will not be stressful when you have the peace of God.

Weakness to Wellness

God created our bodies to be recoupable. Weakness at any age can be overcome. We get weak from poor diet and lack of exercise. When I started exercising at age sixty-four, I had my doubts that I could build muscle because of my age. Then I read an article about a strength training study done at a nursing home with patients in their eighties and nineties.[12]

These patients were characterized as having dropped heads, rounded shoulders, and curved backs. Most had low back pain and spent the majority of their time in bed, chairs, or wheelchairs. They went through a fourteen-week period of strength training consisting of two sessions a week of fifteen to twenty minutes of exercise. Physical therapists worked with each patient to keep their exercises in a safe range. The results were, on average, that their leg strength increased 80 percent, their upper body strength increased by almost 40 percent, joint flexibility increased 30 percent, and improved functional independence measure rose by almost 15 percent. All of the participants exhibited better physical and mental fitness, more endurance, and less lower back pain.[13]

One patient no longer needed the back brace she used for a compression fracture. All of the patients had increased muscle strength, and some spent less time in wheelchairs. The patients began to look forward to the exercise classes because they enjoyed the results. One patient had such good results that she left the nursing home to rejoin her husband. These patients became mobile enough to regain their ability to do walking, washing, dressing, brushing, combing, and other activities. The nursing home experienced a reduction in the cost of care for these patients of almost $40,000 per year.[14]

Our bodies are made by God, and He does not make dysfunctional bodies. He makes them with the inherent ability to function at any age. We become weak, immobile, and sick because of the curse of sin that allowed sickness and death to enter. This is a natural reality, not a kingdom reality; in the kingdom of God we have been redeemed from the curse. We can be strong and healthy at any age if we allow our mind to be renewed to this kingdom reality. Retirement is an old-age plan in the world, but no retirement is needed in the kingdom of God. We do not come to a certain age and then the Holy Spirit leaves us. He does not say, "Well, I am going now because you are too old for Me." When Jesus said that the kingdom of God dwells within us, He did not put an age limit on that spiritual reality.

When we were doing training in Spokane for people who wanted to be a part of our prayer team in the healing rooms there, two retired nuns attended. During our introduction, they told us they had retired but had heard about what was happening in the healing rooms and wanted to be part of it. They said, "We may be retired, but we came to be refired." Both ladies were in their eighties and still had an attitude that said, "We are not finished serving God. There is more that God wants to do with us."

We have been so blessed to see these ladies, filled with the Holy Spirit and fire, doing the work of the kingdom. God wants the weak to be strengthened at any age. We are to run the race with strength not weakness, as I mentioned earlier:

> Therefore, strengthen the hands that are weak and the knees that are feeble, and make straight paths for your feet, so that the limb which is lame may not be put out of joint, but rather be healed.
> —HEBREWS 12:12–13

While these verses are an analogy for the spiritual condition of believers, they give us the picture of the literal reality of physical healing. Health issues can cause us to feel weak spiritually as well as physically. We need to minister the truth of God in each situation to be strengthened in body, soul, and spirit. Physical illness can discourage us so that we cannot run the race God sets before us. We are exhorted to "lay aside every encumbrance and the sin which so easily entangles us, and let us run with endurance the race that is set before us" (Heb. 12:1).

Being unhealthy and physically weak is an "encumbrance" that can so easily entangle you. You need spiritual strength and a healthy body to run the race set before you. When you are strong and healthy physically, you will not have a weak limb that can be injured. How many weak people have you seen who have broken a joint because of a fall? When you strengthen yourself spiritually and physically, your path will be straight; you can run the race with endurance.

A Lifestyle

Earlier I mentioned that my life, which was out of order, determined the lifestyle that I lived. Now my lifestyle determines my life. As I explained earlier, lifestyle is how we operate; we do wrong things, and they impact every area of our life in a wrong way. I came to realize that my lifestyle would either extend my life or it would take my life. When my life was out of order, I ate wrong and did not exercise at all; that was my lifestyle. My circumstances dictated my quality of life when my lifestyle was not good.

Because of my wrong lifestyle, my circumstances eventually became high blood pressure, cholesterol problems, and heart disease. I felt like I was living under my circumstances, limited by my health condition. I just accepted the fact that this is where things were for me. That was absolutely true. I was under my circumstances, out of control of my physical well-being. In the process of recouping my health, I discovered that when I was out of control, the enemy was in control; when God is in control, the enemy is out of control.

When our lifestyles are led by God, our lives come into kingdom order. A kingdom lifestyle does not focus on the temporal but on the eternal. We must realize how important our physical, as well as our spiritual, health is to the Holy Spirit. Then we will consider His eternal purposes, not just the temporal goals, especially when it comes to eating and exercise. The Holy Spirit wants to flow His divine life through His vessel all the time. As we submit to Him, we do not eat well just for the moment; we do not exercise for temporal gain; we do not walk in the Spirit for temporal results but to fulfill His eternal purposes.

> Surely goodness and lovingkindness will follow me all the days of my life, and I will dwell in the house of the LORD forever.
>
> —PSALM 23:6

The good news is that the Holy Spirit will never run out of provision for us. All the days of our lives will be filled with His goodness and loving-kindness as we choose to follow Him. God promises that we dwell with Him forever. It is in the dwelling that His benefits come to us. He also promises that we can enjoy long life: "With a long life I will satisfy him and let him see My salvation" (Ps. 91:16). A long satisfied life is a life that is full and has plenty. Our life is good when we choose to follow the Holy Spirit in our lifestyle. Our way of living is only fruitful when it is yielded to the Spirit of God.

As I mentioned earlier, the apostle Paul had so yielded his life to the Holy Spirit that he could declare:

> I have been crucified with Christ; and it is no longer I who live, but Christ lives in me; and the life which I now live in the flesh I live by faith in the Son of God, who loved me and gave Himself up for me.
>
> —GALATIANS 2:20

As believers, we are the temple of the Holy Spirit to reflect His life in the earth. That means our lifestyle belongs to God. We must learn to say with Paul, "I no longer live, but it is now Christ who lives in me."

The fact that we become the host of Christ's presence, His dwelling place, puts a demand upon our responsibility for stewardship of our lives—body, soul, and spirit.

When someone important comes to your house, doesn't it put a demand on you to put your best foot forward? Do you want the house to be in good order? Similarly, if you are the "house" and the Spirit of God is coming to dwell there, shouldn't you get His house in order? And should that orderliness be temporary or permanent? It is your lifestyle that will determine the permanent condition of your "house." What is your house to look like? It is meant to reflect the will of God in the earth. When you no longer live, then you submit to Christ, who takes over and lives in you. Then you live by faith in the Son of God. It is this transformation that puts your lifestyle into kingdom order.

Kingdom Strength

God wants you to be strong in spirit, in mind, and in body. I have noticed that I lose strength when I do things my way rather than God's way. When I had things out of order, I had dis-order. When I ate wrong, I got a wrong result. Every time I got out of God's will, I got into my will—and my will always produced failure. I understood the psalmist's cry:

> My strength has failed because of my iniquity, and my body has wasted away.
>
> —PSALM 31:10

The word *iniquity* refers to depravity or perversity, corrupt and opposed to what is good.[15] I was opposing the good when I desired unhealthy foods and ate all the time. As a result of my unhealthy lifestyle, my body began to waste away. I knew when I was out of shape and wasting away that I needed help. But I did not have the strength to do it myself. I placed my confidence in God's strength within me; as weak as I was, I knew I could depend on God's strength. The apostle Paul expressed his confidence in the indwelling power of Christ:

> I will rather boast about my weaknesses, so that the power of Christ may dwell in me.
>
> —2 Corinthians 12:9

I had to give up trying in my own strength to diet and exercise, which always resulted in failure. I had to admit that this pursuit of health was not about me; it was about God dwelling in me, who would strengthen me for His purposes. It was about the power of Christ that would conquer my weakness. To embrace this reality, I had to submit what I had to God: my weakness. Then I could receive the promised truth: "for when I am weak, then I am strong" (2 Cor. 12:10).

In other words, when we submit our weakness to God, by His Spirit within us we become strong. Again, Paul exhorted believers to "be strong in the Lord and in the strength of *His* might" (Eph. 6:10, emphasis added). The sustaining power we need to maintain good health is to obey the Word of God that tells us:

> Seek the Lord and His strength; seek His face continually.
>
> —Psalm 105:4

> He is their strength in time of trouble.
>
> —Psalm 37:39

Though God has promised to be our strength in time of trouble, He also says we are to seek Him continually, not just when we are in trouble. We are to live in Him continually. Not only are we to partner with God, but also God wants to partner with us. God created us for partnership. He would not occupy us with His Spirit if He was not interested in intimate relationship with us. By His occupation we are given a divine immune defense system. He strengthens us to resist the evil one and his plans for our destruction. As we continually draw near to God, we receive strength to resist the enemy, and he has to flee (James 4:7). The Lord becomes our strong defense against every tactic of the enemy:

> The LORD is their strength, and He is a saving defense to His anointed.
>
> —PSALM 28:8

He can be a saving defense to us because He is greater than any destructive force that comes against us. God designed us to be strong. Sin made us weak. Then God redeemed us and moved into our spirit so that we could be strong once again. The prayer of the apostle Paul for believers reflects God's attitude and desire for us:

> [To be] strengthened with all power, according to His glorious might, for the attaining of all steadfastness and patience; joyously giving thanks to the Father, who has qualified us to share in the inheritance of the saints in Light.
>
> —COLOSSIANS 1:11–12

God wants to provide all power to us, by His might, so that we can run the race with steadfastness or endurance. He wants us to live in thanksgiving for our relationship with Him through which He has qualified us, by the blood of Jesus, to share in "His inheritance with the saints in Light." The Greek word for *light* means "to shine as fire or to make manifest."[16] God wants to strengthen His people in order to manifest His will and love through them into the world. This is His kingdom coming on earth as it is in heaven.

Exercise

I know many people do not like the word *exercise*. When I complained about exercise, the Holy Spirit said to me, "You only have one body.

You mess it up, we are both out." I thought, "That is really true. I only have one body, and I need to take care of it. Without exercise, there is no strength. I need strength to serve God and enjoy life." As I have said, God did not create man to be weak. God is not weak, and He is in us to make us strong. Just as by the Holy Spirit we know His Word and become spiritually strong when we exercise it, so when we exercise in the natural, we become physically strong.

God gave our bodies muscle tissue to provide us with physical strength. As God created us, we are a spirit man, who has a soul (mind, will, emotions) and lives in a body. God created all three aspects of our personhood. We have to steward all three by the power of God. When we strengthen our physical body through exercise, we move the spirit and mind according to the will of God. In other words, we take responsibility to steward our spirit and mind, linking them to God's purpose.

The physical man is not only the temple of the Holy Spirit; it is also the temple of the spirit and soul of man. All three—body, soul, and spirit—are designed by God. All three are redeemed by God. All three are called by God. And all three are led by God. But all three are exercised by man. Stewardship must be applied to the spirit, mind, and body. When all three are properly exercised, we discover that the Lord becomes a refuge and a tower of strength for us (Ps. 61:3). In 2 Corinthians 12:10 the apostle Paul declared, "When I am weak, then I am strong" because Christ's power is perfected in weakness (v. 9). When we choose to allow Christ to rule in us, we become a strong tower against the onslaught of the enemy.

There is value in bodily discipline: "For bodily discipline is only of little profit, but godliness is profitable for all things, since it holds promise for the present life and also for the life to come" (1 Tim. 4:8). Some quote this verse to justify their lack of exercise. But it does not say that bodily discipline or exercise is *not* profitable. On the contrary, it says it is profitable, just not as profitable as godliness, for one obvious reason. Bodily discipline only benefits us here; godliness will profit us both here and in the life to come.

In the previous verse Paul exhorted Timothy to "discipline yourself for the purpose of godliness" (v. 7). Our purpose for bodily exercise should be to support our pursuit of godliness. Our measure of godliness is determined by the measure of God in us. Our purpose should be to maintain our spirit, our mind, and our body in as good a shape as possible for the work of the Holy Spirit to succeed in us and through us.

We can follow this discipline throughout our years of life; it is not something we do only when we are young. All the years of our life are valuable to God. God created us to age well. We need to embrace a kingdom perspective of aging. Aging is not about getting old, out of shape, weak, and falling apart. Aging is about accumulation of wisdom and knowledge of God that is added to the godly with every year of added life. It is about increasing value, not decreasing it each year. God will not change or cancel His plans for us when we get older.

We cancel them only when we believe we cannot do anything more. There is no cancellation of godly living in a kingdom that is without end. We need to embrace the promise of the Word for our old age:

> Even to your old age I will be the same, and even to your graying years I will bear you! I have done it, and I will carry you; and I will bear you and I will deliver you.
> —ISAIAH 46:4

God promises to be the same to you in your early years and your latter years. He carried you then, and He will carry you into old age. He is the God of deliverance from the beginning to the end of your life. The benefits of His will are the same every year He gives to you to live.

> My son, do not forget my teaching, but let your heart keep my commandments; for length of days and years of life and peace they will add to you.
>
> —PROVERBS 3:1–2

Throughout our lives we are to keep the will of God diligently in our hearts. It is His will fulfilled in us that gives us length of days and a long life.

Counting the Cost

Before I could begin this journey of walking in health, I had to consider the cost. I knew I had to develop a good nutritional diet and exercise program. This adjustment would require some hard changes in my life. Then I thought about my alternative options. When I suffered the heart attack, it required a huge adjustment in my life that would ultimately be very positive. I realized I needed to make a commitment to pursue health.

In order to justify the cost for my pursuit of health, I had to see the *value* of what living a healthy life offered me. I began to understand that the value of having a healthy body not only benefits me, but it also benefits the Holy Spirit, who dwells in me. As I committed myself to pursuing health, I began to have renewed energy for my ministry in our healing rooms. I was surprised to find I had strength that I had not experienced in thirty years. I could walk up stairs without being out of breath.

Another added benefit was that my clothes began to fit me correctly. (It is OK with God for us to look good.) I found I no longer needed two sets of clothes—one for when my weight was up and one for when it was down. On my journey to health I also discovered greater value in our marriage. Michelle and I could do more things together because we had the energy to do them. When we traveled to do conferences, we had more energy to minister together. We began to take walks together and discovered a new love to be outside doing things. We discovered added value not only in our marriage but also for our future together. When my health was poor, I did not like thinking about the future. I felt a constant anxiety about growing old, losing quality of life, and then dying. In my mind I found myself constantly trying to hang on to the "now" because I did not know what my future held health wise.

With my newly found health, I also had the value of being able to give a testimony of God's power and faithfulness in my life. The Holy Spirit said to me, "You cannot bring this message of health to the body of Christ unless you *become* the message." When we receive the benefit of health that Jesus provided through redemption, we are a living example of the will of God being done in earth as it is in heaven. We reflect the grace and power of the Holy Spirit within us to help us overcome our weakness by the renewing of our minds and to walk in His provision of health: body, soul, and spirit.

Avoiding the "easy way"

Sure, there is a price to pay and we must consider the cost, but the value of pursuing health far exceeds the alternative awaiting the outcome of our poor health. Living in good health is a way of life; it is a lifestyle that can improve the quality of our life and extend it for many years.

Have you ever wondered why it is so easy to do things that are not good for you and so difficult to do things that are? It was always easy for me to eat things that were unhealthy, yet so difficult to eat things that were good for me. When my mind was set on my flesh, eating wrong things was easy. Only when I set my mind on the Spirit did I have the power to eat good things. When we value what God values, then we can move into stewardship. Stewardship of our health requires us to possess or have control over our own vessel or body:

That each of you know how to possess his own vessel in sanctification and honor.

—1 Thessalonians 4:4

We cannot possess our own vessel in honor when our mind is set to indulge our flesh. Instead we will be given to lustful passions and to craving things that run counter to God's will. Our flesh will yield to every temptation, even while we are pursuing health. This focus on satisfying our fleshly desire will bring failure in our diet and exercise program. We must determine to possess our life by submitting it to Christ. Then we will be successful and become an example to others in order that they can achieve a healthy life as well. And we will function in our spiritual endowment given to each believer in Christ:

As each one has received a special gift, employ it in serving one another as good stewards of the manifold grace of God.

—1 Peter 4:10

Need for endurance

For you have need of endurance, so that when you have done the will of God, you may receive what was promised.

—Hebrews 10:36

After beginning my journey to health, I began to realize my need for endurance. To value our life is to value His life that is in us. When I recognized that my health had value, I began to gain confidence that I could develop the endurance to pursue optimal health successfully. With that endurance the temptation to eat unhealthy foods could be overcome. That did not mean I could not have a piece of cake on a special occasion. But it did mean that I could no longer make every occasion *special*.

During my pursuit of health, no matter where I went, there seemed to be temptation that required me to exercise endurance. Everywhere

I went I needed confidence and endurance to withstand the temptation to eat the wrong foods I saw—at the office, at the fast-food restaurant, at the mini-mart, at the dinner house, and at the supermarket. Temptation results from your desires for something with which you have had a relationship. I had a strong love relationship with all these wrong foods, and I found it was hard to get delivered from something that I love. To do so meant I had to break the relationship. I had to love my relationship with the Holy Spirit more than that which I had with food. I could not receive the promise of health until I built up my endurance to overcome the temptation of wrong foods.

I knew God wanted me to be in good health according to His will (3 John 2). I needed endurance to achieve that goal. As hard as I tried, I could not muster up enough endurance to get there. Over the years, as I mentioned, my wife and I dieted and lost weight only to gain it back again. It was a losing battle. Only when we began to partner with the Holy Spirit did we receive the power and grace to endure so that we could succeed in living in health.

We had to become doers of the Word, not just hearers (James 1:22). It is so interesting to see how our bodies respond to a healthy lifestyle. It is as though they say, "Thank you for doing that." When you think about it, our bodies that are filled with life initially go through much trauma when we eat wrong and do not exercise. The body has to constantly overwork to try to maintain a healthy immune system against sickness. Without giving the body the nutrition and exercise it needs, it cannot sustain resistance to sickness and disease.

When you eat healthily and exercise, you are doing what is normal to your body. Your body then begins to restore itself. Proper nutrition feeds the cells, making them healthy. Exercise begins to restore muscle and increases blood flow for healthy joints, vessels, heart, and lung capacity. Your body begins to provide a better accommodation for your spirit and mind. Then your spirit and mind, with the support of a healthy body, can be released from focusing on pain and misery to focus on spiritual increase. You allow the Holy Spirit to flow through you to fulfill His will in your life, unhindered by the physical issues you once suffered.

When the physical body is in trauma of pain or sickness, spiritual capacity is diminished. Isn't that the goal of the enemy, to diminish our spiritual capacity? It is not only physical trauma that can trip us up, but emotional trauma as well. When we have soul wounds from situations that have caused trauma, it is difficult to focus on our pursuit of health. It is important to walk in forgiveness with people who have hurt us in the past. This is part of the cost we have to pay to live in health. It is not just the body that is to be healthy, but the spirit and mind as well. If we are going to partner with the Holy Spirit, we must be willing to obey His conviction when He show us wounds and unforgiveness; we must address them by repenting of unforgiveness and bitterness and asking God to heal our hearts. Remember, Jesus warned:

> Whenever you stand praying, *forgive*, if you have anything against anyone, so that your Father who is in heaven will also forgive you your transgressions. But if you do not forgive, neither will your Father who is in heaven forgive your transgressions.
> —Mark 11:25–26, emphasis added

This is huge. Too often people are battling weight and health issues that are caused by deeper issues of wounding, which results in unforgiveness. If you cannot overcome the cause, you cannot overcome the symptoms of the problem. God's Word teaches to forgive as Jesus forgave you. If you do not, you lose God's support through disobedience.

Often, it is pride that keeps us from obeying God's commands. He says He resists the proud (James 4:6). Pride does not give you a breakthrough; it leads to a fall. If you are to be led by the Spirit, then you must obey the Spirit when He shines His light on unforgiveness or any other sin you are harboring. You cannot get delivered from something you are hanging on to.

We see people who come to the healing rooms for deliverance or divine healing, but they do not see their breakthrough because they are hanging on to the very issues that caused the problem in the first place. When God says to forgive, it is not a suggestion. You cannot disobey God and expect to receive His blessing at the same time.

Quality of Life

It is difficult to overstate the value there is in living a life of health. Being in good health provides quality of life for every day of your life. It is your quality of life that provides strength, as a believer, to fulfill your destiny. You cannot bring His kingdom will to earth if you are not living in His kingdom. The kingdom of God provides everything needed for healing and health so that you can enjoy the quality of abundant life He came to give:

> I came that they might have life, and might have it abundantly.
> —JOHN 10:10

In the next chapter my wife, Michelle, will share with you her struggle against gluttony and her testimony of how she was able to endure and to receive the abundant life Jesus came to give to her.

Chapter 8

OVERCOMING THE SPIRIT OF GLUTTONY

By Michelle Pierce

*You cannot be an overcomer unless you
have something to overcome.*

This chapter is about my personal struggle with food and the weight issues I suffered as a result. I want to share with you how I found the way out of my lifelong dilemma and was delivered from a spirit of gluttony by the power of God. As you share my journey from failure to freedom, from bondage to food to a life of health, I want you to receive hope for your situation. You can also be a free person no matter how cruel the bondage is that keeps you from enjoying the abundant life Jesus came to give you.

My Family

I was raised in Redding, California, and after I married Cal, we raised our children there as well. I am the oldest child of my parents, and I have a brother and sister. I know that my struggle with food started when I was young. Parents often say their children take after one parent or the other. Well, I took after my dad, which was positive in some ways but had its negative aspects also.

Perhaps you are familiar with the classic study of temperaments that divides most personalities into one of four types: sanguine, choleric, melancholic, and phlegmatic. Most people's personalities fit dominantly into one of these general types, each having decidedly different character traits, which influence their approach to life. When I took this typical temperament evaluation many years ago during a class given at my church, it revealed that my personality fit best with the traits of the sanguine, including the negative characteristics of that temperament type.

I learned that the person with a sanguine temperament is fairly extroverted. These personality types tend to enjoy social gatherings and making new friends. They also tend to be quite loud, letting people know they are in the room. They are usually quite creative and often given to daydreaming. Sanguine people can be very sensitive, compassionate, and thoughtful. They are very people oriented, talkative, and not shy. They are friendly and make good friends—often making lifelong friends. Those are some of the positive traits they share.

However, on the negative side, sanguine personalities generally struggle with following through to finish a task they begin. In fact, they may have ten projects lying around, all in various stages of completion. Because the priority of life for the sanguine personality is to have fun, they may lose interest quickly when pursuing a hobby, for example, when it ceases to be fun. They tend to be chronically late, forgetful, and, more often than not, can be known for their sarcasm. Because they are so people oriented, they do not like to be alone. However, some alone time is crucial for those of this temperament in order to learn to seek the Lord.

I recognized, after my study of these classic temperaments, that my dad was a delight sanguine. He was funny and had a great laugh. I remember in high school the neighborhood kids saying that my dad woke them up every morning with his loud laugh. He was very creative and often daydreamed. However, he was not sensitive, compassionate, or thoughtful.

My dad was a successful DJ for our local radio station. He did the morning show and was so good at doing the commercials that everyone wanted him to do their commercials during his show, which left little time for playing songs. His sanguine personality made him a natural for this type of work.

However, he also had an addictive personality, which means he was more than normally susceptible to addictive behavior. He was the leader of a country and western band that played in dance halls on weekends. In that rowdy environment, Dad started drinking, he said, to help him sleep. I remember once that we kids were hiding in our bedroom because Dad came home drunk. I climbed up to the top bunk bed to hide with my brother. When Dad came into the bedroom, my brother sat up. I was so frightened because my daddy was yelling. I don't remember what it was about, and I didn't know if we were going to get spanked or not.

On another occasion, when I was in high school, Dad asked me to put more whiskey into his glass. Instead, I filled it with tea. You guessed it; he did not think that was funny, but I thought it was very funny. Dad drank for many years, but mostly at night to go to sleep. Finally, after I had graduated from high school, Dad was able to break his addiction to alcohol. He just stopped drinking. But it wasn't long until he was engaged in his next addiction: food. He just started eating everything in sight, all the time.

Now I realize that my dad believed life revolved around him. What he wanted or felt he needed was what the family had to make happen. Life at home became more and more difficult as his "needs" took a toll on the family finances. All of this was very hard on my mother, who worked very hard as a waitress to try to keep our family together. My mother made clothes for my sister and me when we were in grammar school. And she was the one who fixed anything in the home, like plumbing problems. I loved my mother very much and blamed my dad for the life my mom and we kids had to live.

Dad was very gifted. If something interested him, he would go after it and learn everything about it. But after he had mastered whatever project he was doing, he grew tired of it and looked for something else. For example, he built his own computer and a ham radio with which he talked to people from all over the world. Later he started a photograph business and built a dark room in our home. He bought a horse and taught it to do tricks and would ride him in the parades. After that he developed a group of riders, called the Oregon Trail Riders, men and women who would square dance on their horses during half time at rodeos.

Once he decided he wanted to learn to paint. He learned to paint by watching expensive tapes, purchasing a lot of them that taught him to paint with watercolors and oils. He became a very good artist; I still have some of his paintings. His next venture was to learn to tie flies for fishing. Again, he bought more tapes that taught him to master tying flies. After that he wanted to learn to whittle on wood. He made some beautiful walking sticks that my siblings and I have in our homes.

The last thing my dad did was to learn to master the art of "rendering," which is the process of generating an image from a model or models by means of computer programs. In this way he would create scene files of people and places and upload them on his computer using very expensive software programs. I remember that he made a scene of a church chapel that people could access from their computers and "go there" to pray or to ask for prayer. These pursuits created a financial hardship on our family, which also affected my feelings toward my dad. To begin with, he needed two computers for this venture, and it seemed there was always another expensive software program that would make it easier for him.

During my high school years, I sometimes felt I did not love my dad, which was very hard for me to admit, because I had loved him dearly. I do not believe my dad ever understood how his actions affected the family. As an adult believer, I understand better now and have made peace in my heart with my childhood. I have forgiven my dad, and we enjoyed a good relationship in the latter years of his life. I have learned how important it is to our walk with the Lord to forgive those who hurt us deeply, because unforgiveness holds us back from being all God wants us to be.

My sister and brother and I have all had issues with food. I now believe some of our problems have been a result of generational curses, enemy strongholds in our family passed from one generation to another. Both my dad's and my mother's families struggled with major weight issues. Another factor contributing to my problems were harsh words spoken to me as a child that hurt my spirit. I learned to just "stuff" my hurts and disappointments inside so no one would know how I felt. Of course, these unresolved conflicts led to many problems later in life. I had a hard time feeling good about myself. I did not think I was smart like my father, and I did not like to work like my mother. These feelings of unworthiness made it difficult to like myself and accept myself for the person God made me to be.

Perhaps some of you can relate to these childhood conflicts; some may have suffered more than I have in your childhood; others may have had awesome childhood upbringing. Yet you may still be trying to understand why you are experiencing health issues related to food and being overweight.

I have shared some of my story because it reveals some root causes of "unhealth" in my mind and spirit that needed to be healed, causes which affected my physical health and the wrong lifestyle choices I made regarding food. Remember, the real goal is to pursue health in body, mind, and spirit.

My Marriage

When I was a sophomore in high school my family moved ten miles out of Redding to Palo Cedro. I started attending the new high school, and it was there that I met Cal. We started dating and went together until I graduated in June of 1964. On August 22, 1964, we married. I was not aware at the time of all the emotional hurts and wounding I carried into the marriage. I did not recognize the ways I had been wounded in my childhood or what effect they would have on my marriage relationship.

Just as we inherit the way we look on the outside, we can also inherit some family traits that are not good for us. We often see in families that have had generations troubled with alcohol issues, for example, that these traits are passed on to the next generation. Generational curses are sins that are passed down through the family, according to Deuteronomy 5:9–10. While my brother struggled with addiction to alcohol, I struggled with food addiction.

I had never heard of the spiritual reality of generational curses. Yet there they were, packed in my "suitcases." All my emotional baggage followed me into my marriage. My issues with being overweight started creating tension early in our marriage. I think I went on diet pills during our first year of marriage. Back then the doctors gave out lots of pills to help people lose weight. They worked for a while, but then the weight would seem to just come back on.

My Children

Cal and I had two sons, Carl and David. When David turned five, we decided to adopt a little girl. Our daughter, Jaime Michelle, was born in Seoul, South Korea; she came into our family when she was seven months old. When we adopted Jaime, I remember being excited that she would not have to suffer with the family issues of being overweight as I did because she did not have my genes. I forgot that genes are just a part of the problem; the environment in which you are raised is a big factor in how you relate to food, for example. I only tell you that Jaime is our adopted daughter to explain my feelings about my own personality issues. Jaime is a part of Cal and me and even has some of our attributes. I thank the Lord daily that Jaime is *our* daughter.

At the same time we adopted Jaime, our son David was diagnosed with Duchenne muscular dystrophy. I can remember driving home from the medical center in Sacramento, California, saying to Cal, "I am so glad we know the Lord." David had a friend who had cancer and died. I knew, from the prognosis, that David had at least eighteen years or more for the Lord to heal him. You see, I believed it was up to Jesus to heal in His time; I did not understand that He had provided healing through His death on the cross. What I prayed was, "God, if it is Your will, please heal David, but if he is not going to be healed, please take him home to heaven before he gets too bad."

David was a teenager when his disease began to make his life very difficult. When he was nineteen, he had a mild heart attack due to his struggle with fluid buildup, which made breathing very difficult. Doctors prescribed diuretics to help his body handle the fluids and ease his breathing. David went home to be with the Lord on February 2, 1992; he was twenty years old.

Many times people would tell us how great we were to raise our son David with muscular dystrophy (MD). I never felt that it was hard; David was such an awesome young man. He never asked, "Why me?" He never even dreamed about being out of the wheelchair. David was always happy as a boy. When he was sixteen, he had an encounter with the Lord that changed his life dramatically. After that divine encounter David prayed all the time; he read his Bible every night. He really was a blessing to our family. I know now that as I was raising David, I pushed down the heartache of the possibility of losing him someday. It was just another thing that I stuffed, turning again to food for comfort.

Chronic Weight Issues

I had been raised Catholic. In 1973 the charismatic movement was invading the denominational churches, including the Catholic Church. Someone told us about it, and we decided to check it out. We both rededicated our lives to Jesus, and Cal soon became a leader of the group in the local Catholic church. Later, in 1974, we began attending Bethel Church in Redding and still consider it our home church.

During our marriage Cal and I have had some rough times because of my struggle with food. I knew that Cal did not want a wife who was overweight. So I was continually trying one diet after another to lose weight. I remember one diet I went on that required me to drink six quarts of water a day and eat only 500 calories a day. Cal paid me ten dollars for each pound I lost. When I lost ten pounds, he gave me one hundred dollars. Once I lost fifty pounds, and he took me on a cruise.

But when the diet was over, I started to eat again, and all the weight came back. I have probably tried every diet you can name—and more. During one of our difficult discussions about why I could not keep the weight off, I remember telling Cal I felt as out of control as an alcoholic; there was more truth to that than I realized.

Drastic measures

I remember one time trying to get an appointment with a psychiatrist because I just could not stop eating the wrong kinds of food. Instead I went to my regular doctor, and he prescribed antidepressants. I brought them home but could not bring myself to take them. I felt that as a Christian I should be seeking the Lord for answers instead of pills, and I did that for a while.

Then, in 1979, I heard about a procedure involving stapling the stomach to help with weight loss. I was excited because I just knew that this was the answer to all my problems. My marriage would be better, my self-esteem would be better, and my life would be better. I talked Cal into letting me have the operation, even though it was considered a very extreme measure for losing weight.

In order to qualify for the operation, I needed to be one hundred pounds over the proper weight for my body size. I wasn't. So, to qualify, I would need to gain thirty-five pounds. Surprisingly, trying to gain weight was not that much fun. I got sick of eating the doughnuts, ice cream, and other such foods. I know; I could not believe it either, but it was true. When I reached the qualifying weight, I went to Sacramento, California, to have the operation.

After the operation Cal came into the room to see me. I think for the first time he realized that I was doing all of this to please him, to be the wife he wanted me to be. On his way home to Redding with our children, the Lord had a talk with him about how he had been treating me over these many years. After that encounter, our marriage was so much better, even though I eventually started gaining the weight back. It does not matter what drastic means you use to lose weight; the reality is that if you eat more calories than you burn, you will gain weight.

Deceptive tricks

Hiding food started when I was young; then for many years after I was married, I hid food from Cal. It was awful when he would find the candy I had hidden—or my favorite, the small powdered doughnuts. I would get up early before Cal did to have my coffee and doughnuts so that he would not know I ate them. Sometimes I cannot believe the things I did to hide my eating from Cal. You would think I would figure out that he would know I was eating because I kept getting larger. Then the realization would hit—I was going to have to lose weight again.

I have also had problems with addiction in other areas besides food. Webster's dictionary defines *addiction* as "the state of being enslaved to a habit or practice or to something that is psychologically or physically habit-forming, as narcotics, to such an extent that its cessation causes severe trauma."[1] I had started watching soap operas when I was still living with my parents. After I married and started raising our children, I began watching them again. I think I watched four or five different stories every day. During the commercials I would do a little house cleaning. Otherwise, I sat to watch my soaps.

Then when Cal and I came to the Lord, we sold our TV—no more watching soaps. However, we eventually bought another TV, and I started watching soap operas again—only two programs this time. I knew they were not good to be watching, and I was finally able to quit watching them. It is wonderful to realize now, that if I happen to see one on the TV, I get sick to my stomach. From my place of freedom I cannot believe that I watched them for such a long time.

During an especially hard time in our lives with financial problems and with David's illness, I started reading Harlequin romance books. I do not remember why, but I do know that to me they were little books that always seemed to end happily. I did not want to read what I called "trashy novels." I was convinced the Harlequin books were not like that. Yet I hid them from my friends so they would not know I read them. Now, when I think about my actions during that time, it is hard to believe I could deceive myself in that way.

Our Move to Spokane

When Bill Johnson became the pastor of our church, he brought much needed change to our lives. We had become a very "religious" church. That is, we acted one way in church but lived differently at home. I have to admit that I had become the number one gossip of the church. I am not proud of that, but it was true. After the Holy Spirit brought revival to our church through Pastor Bill's anointed ministry, Cal and I experienced real change in our lives.

Cal was really on fire for the things of God, but I held back. I agreed with all that was happening at church and in my husband's life, but I wasn't sure I wanted to give all of me to Christ. I didn't understand the great grace of God, that He really loved me and accepted me just as I am, extra pounds and all. I am thankful that, as a believer, I had the Holy Spirit, who could teach me and guide me so that I could finally turn my life completely over to Him.

A year or so later, the Lord spoke to Cal that it was time for us to move. Cal had a call on his life and needed to find out what it was, and sometimes that requires moving. He felt God opening a door for us to move to Spokane, Washington. The first house we rented belonged to the Friends Church. It had been the home of their pastor. Since their current pastor had her own home, it was available for rent. Instinctively I knew that I could not bring the Harlequin books into this house that had been dedicated to God's servants, so I stopped reading them. To make sure I didn't go back to reading those books, I would not go down the grocery store aisles where they were displayed. In that way I did not let the enemy entice me to pick them up again.

I really believed that God was setting me up for something big. Besides living in a home dedicated to pastors, the street on which we lived was called "G Street." I began calling it "God Street," sensing that our relocating in Spokane was definitely the will of God for Cal and me.

In Redding, I had worked at the Montgomery Ward's department store in the jewelry department. I was able to transfer to the jewelry department of a Montgomery Ward's store located in Spokane. I was very excited because this store was so much larger than the one in

Redding. I began to love this big city; I grew up in a small town and was fascinated with all I saw in the big city.

After we had lived in Spokane a year and a half, God called Cal to reopen the healing rooms that John G. Lake had started decades earlier. He went first to the southeast corner of Howard and Riverside, where John Lake's healing ministry was located from 1915 to 1920. I told Cal that it was fine with me to open a healing room as long as he did not take any money from our incomes. (Cal worked part-time for the forest service in Coeur D'Alene, Idaho.)

We had known financial difficulties from time to time in our marriage. When we lived in Redding, Cal built office buildings there. Depending on the economy, we were either doing great financially or faltering badly when the construction business faltered. During our bad economic times, our marriage suffered, and I continued to seek comfort in food. This had been a habit all of my life.

Even as a Christian, I did not learn how to receive the comfort of the Holy Spirit that Jesus promised. When we moved to Spokane, I was hopeful that things were going to be different. I had no idea the dramatic changes the Lord had awaiting for us in the days ahead. I have been a Christian for more than thirty years, but it was not until we moved to Spokane that I really began to grow in my relationship with the Lord.

I remembered Pastor Bill Johnson teaching us how a person who does not have an intimate relationship with the Lord may think they do because of the godly atmosphere that surrounds them in the church. I knew that I did not pray or read the Word as I should; I let Cal do that. In fact, I did not realize then that I had set my husband in the place the Lord should have had in my life. For example, if Cal was struggling in his walk with the Lord, fear gripped my heart; if our income plummeted, I became afraid because I looked to Cal as my provider. Praise the Lord, I have grown in my personal relationship with God so that I now know who my provider is and my peace does not depend on how Cal is doing.

When Cal was led to open the healing rooms, I was not ready to follow him into that ministry. It was OK for him, but I was not ready to give my all to the call of God on *his* life. I was still trusting in the income I made from my employment rather than putting my trust in the provision of the Lord. Actually, I now realize that *trust* on every level has been a big issue in my life. Faced with the challenge of Cal's new ministry, it took some time for me to say *yes* to the Lord about being a part of it.

When I finally surrendered to trusting God, I quit my job; I have to admit, I was scared. I had to actually imagine myself drawing a line in the sand and then deliberately stepping over the line saying, "Yes, Lord, I trust You." In my walk with the Lord, I have had to do that on many occasions regarding finances, relationships, or whatever situation in which the Lord has shown me that I need to trust Him.

It seems to me that God had a sense of humor in placing me in the Healing Rooms Ministries with the title "Codirector" because, as I said, I knew very little of the Word of God. But God, in His infinite wisdom, sent a godly couple from our church in Redding just to be servants to us in this ministry. Because the wife, Marie, was from our church, I felt comfortable with her and drawn to relationship with her. Before long she had become my mentor, teaching me spiritual truths; I call her my spiritual mother. During that time God gave us other godly team members as well who have spoken truth into my life. I love each of them for helping me to grow in God.

Now, when I speak at conferences about my first experience of being part of the Healing Rooms Ministries, I share how excited I was when I first saw "yellow" highlighting in my Bible. I can hear you laughing now, but it was a significant step in my growth in God. Let me explain. I would sit next to friends in church and would see that verses in their Bible were highlighted in yellow; others used blue or green colors to highlight special verses that the Lord had made real to them.

I didn't have any verses highlighted in my Bible in any color. As the Lord put real desire in my heart to know Him and to read His Word, I began to highlight verses that He made real to me. So, when I open my Bible now and see yellow, I am excited because it means that the Lord is speaking to me through His Word. He has been so faithful to continue to teach me and lead me in the ways of the kingdom.

Becoming Aware of the Spirit of Gluttony

When Cal had a dream that he was going to get strong, as he shared earlier, he made a decision to pursue a lifestyle of health. I knew that, as his wife, I was going to have to lose weight—one more time. Of course, in my mind that meant another diet and another failure. I had failed to keep the weight off with every other diet and more drastic measures, so why should I think this time it would be different?

But I decided to join my husband's pursuit of health and started a very strict diet. Of course, I lost weight initially. During this time, I read a book by Diane Hampton called *The Diet Alternative* that taught about a spirit of gluttony.[2] When I saw myself in those pages, for the first time I had hope that I could be free from my lifelong issues with food. I began to understand that I could pray and break the spirit of gluttony over my life, which would set me free from my alcoholic-type addiction to food. Then I would be free to pursue weight loss and be successful in losing and keeping the weight off. I began to search the Scriptures regarding our relationship to food and found much instruction that was helpful for my deliverance. Before I share some of them with you, we need to define clearly the spirit of gluttony.

What is the spirit of gluttony?

What is gluttony? According to Webster's, *gluttony* is defined simply as "excess in eating or drinking."[3] What happens when you are habitually given to gluttony, or any other fleshly bondage, is that the devil takes advantage and energizes your "besetting sin" with a demonic spirit. When the devil observes the signs of gluttony in your life, overeating, eating unhealthily and just for pleasure, it gives the demon of gluttony a legal right of entry to your life, based on your wrong choices. Remember, his goal is to destroy your life by whatever means (John 10:10). Once the destructive habit becomes a part of your life, you may think, "That is the way I am." You may feel out of control, as I did, searching for natural sources of help but not realizing the problem has a spiritual root.

The term *glutton* has come to mean anything for which you have a great capacity; i.e., a glutton for punishment.[4] If you are aware of areas of addictive behavior in your life that harm your physical, emotional, and/or spiritual health, you may have opened the door to an evil spirit of gluttony. A person who is bound by a spirit of gluttony will suffer unnatural eating habits, compulsions, and cravings. Gluttony causes your mind to fantasize about food all the time. Until we recognize that there is a spiritual bondage that has a hold on us, for all our efforts to be free, we are no match for that evil spirit; we will never live in lasting victory over it.

"You will know the truth..." (John 8:32)

I was amazed at what the Holy Spirit began to show me in the Scriptures regarding gluttony. I want to share some of these scriptures that the Lord highlighted for me. There are many more, and I encourage you to search them out for yourself. The scriptures identify gluttony as a sin of idolatry.

> Whose end is destruction, whose god is their belly, and whose glory is in their shame—who set their mind on earthly things.
> —PHILIPPIANS 3:19, NKJV

They warn us not to associate with drunkards or gluttons:

> Do not carouse with drunkards or feast with gluttons, for they are on their way to poverty.
> —PROVERBS 23:19–21, NLT

Did you see that? Drunkards are cited in the verse, along with gluttons, with the command to avoid associating with them. That was striking to me because my dad was an alcoholic and I have been a glutton. I remembered saying to my husband that I felt out of control regarding food just as an alcoholic is out of control with drinking. Yet how many people consider gluttony to be in the same class of debauched living as drunkenness? Both are addictions to a substance, whether alcohol or food. Yet we often minister to the drunkard but not the glutton. Therefore the person dealing with an eating disorder is overlooked and left alone with no help. Somehow we treat gluttony as a more "respectable" sin than we do alcoholism, but this proverb condemns both, citing that both the glutton and the drunkard are on their way to poverty.

The Hebrew word translated as *poverty* is used in a broad sense to mean literal poverty as well as ruin, destruction, and disinheritance.[5] I think the poverty of soul that I suffered from my bondage to gluttony was greater than a lack of finances. I felt so awful about myself that I did not read the Word or pursue other means of grace to find freedom from my plight. Yet I would never have considered my being overweight or addiction to food as bad as being an alcoholic like my father. We need to see the way God sees and accept the fact that both conditions lead to the same destructive end. We must start seeing that we need help just like the person who drinks too much.

As I searched the Scriptures to learn how God viewed my lifelong bondage to food, He was faithful to show me the truth that would set me free. Another scripture the Lord showed me was part of Jesus's parable regarding the seed of the Word falling on good soil and on bad soil:

> As for what was sown among thorns, this is he who hears the Word, but cares of the world and the pleasure and delight and glamour and deceitfulness of riches choke and suffocate the Word, and it yields no fruit.
>
> —MATTHEW 13:22, AMP

This soil filled with thorns was a picture of my life. I went to church and heard the Word taught, but in everyday life I thought about food much more than I ever thought about God. I have learned that when the Lord speaks to me about an area that needs to be brought under His control, I need to repent, without hesitation, and go forward with whatever He is asking of me. Once I hesitate, I open the door for the enemy or my own flesh to speak their desires, which oppose the will of God. This next scripture confirms the power our own evil desires exercise in our life:

> But every person is tempted when he is drawn away, enticed and baited by his own evil desire (lust, passions). Then the evil desire, when it has conceived, gives birth to sin, and sin, when it is fully matured, brings forth death.
>
> —JAMES 1:14–15, AMP

I have learned the hard way that the only voice we should listen to is the Lord's voice, because He has promised that His truth will set us free (John 8:32). The voice of my flesh was so strong that I remember saying, "I don't ask the Holy Spirit what I should eat each day because I don't want to hear the answer." You see, the desire of my flesh was to eat what I wanted when I wanted instead of eating what was good for me and what would bring me health. Obviously I did not have a very close relationship with the Holy Spirit. I purposely kept Him out of that area of my life.

When I first came into the Healing Room Ministries, I would speak very negative words about myself. I felt that if I said it first, other people would not have to think badly about me. I did not realize I was speaking curses upon my own head until the Lord showed me another truth in His Word:

> Death and life are in the power of the tongue, and those who love it will eat its fruit.
>
> —PROVERBS 18:21, NKJV

That is why it is so important to only speak the truth of God, which is life, over ourselves and others. Otherwise we empower the enemy to speak his lies of failure and defeat through us, and we cannot see ourselves as God sees us—already healed and delivered.

Keeping with the analogy of sowing the right seed into good soil, I began to understand this truth also:

> Do not be deceived, God is not mocked; for whatever a man sows, that he will also reap.
>
> —GALATIANS 6:7, NKJV

When we eat in a way that is unhealthy, giving in to the desires of the flesh, the seeds of gluttony are sown into our lives. What have you sown into the soil of your heart? I know I sowed unhappiness, sickness, high cholesterol, and, most importantly, a poor relationship with the Holy Spirit. I had not yielded to His comforting presence or allowed Him to teach me the ways of the Lord. The Lord has promised to help when we call on Him; I just never called Him.

How to Overcome the Spirit of Gluttony

As I began to see the truth of God's Word, it filled me with faith that I could be set free from my lifelong struggle with gluttony. I could overcome this enemy of my life, this bondage to the evil one, and live in freedom health. The first thing I did was repent for yielding to the temptation of lust for food. Then I submitted this area of my life to God and asked Him to help me, through His power, to overcome gluttony. I asked the Holy Spirit to strengthen me against yielding to the spirit of gluttony as I had done for years. I embraced the promise of victory over the devil in the Word: "Therefore submit to God. Resist the devil and he will flee from you" (James 4:7, NKJV).

When Cal shared his dream with me in which he saw himself becoming strong, I had been on another very strict diet and had lost considerable weight. But I knew my track record for losing and than regaining weight over and over again. This time I asked the Holy Spirit how to continue in my weight-loss program and maintain victory over my desire for unhealthy foods. Again I received a wonderful promise from the Word:

> Now this is the confidence that we have in Him, that if we ask anything according to His will, He hears us. And if we know that He hears us, whatever we ask, we know that we have the petitions that we have asked of Him.
> —1 JOHN 5:14–15, NKJV

Because this battle with gluttony has been a lifelong battle, even since my deliverance from the spirit of gluttony, there have been times when I ate more than I needed. When that happens, I have to remember that I am *free* from that spirit; it cannot condemn me or have any hold on me ever again to make me fall back into a familiar habit pattern of eating. It is very important that I not allow overeating to become a new habit going forward. Again, I declare over my life the promise of God's Word that has set me free:

> There is therefore now no condemnation to them which are in Christ Jesus, who walk not after the flesh, but after the Spirit. For the law of the Spirit of life in Christ Jesus hath made me free from the law of sin and death. For what the law could not do, in that it was weak through the flesh, God sending his own Son in the likeness of sinful flesh, and for sin, condemned sin in the flesh: That the righteousness of the law might be fulfilled in us, who walk not after the flesh, but after the Spirit.
>
> —ROMANS 8:1–4, KJV

A work in progress

You are probably familiar with the little cookies some airlines offer as a snack instead of pretzels. Well, I love those little cookies. When Cal and I flew to conferences, I looked forward to eating those special cookies on the airplane. I have actually gotten mad at Cal if he did not take them for his snack, thinking I could have eaten his as well. But one principle I have learned in walking in freedom over gluttony is to give up a favorite food as a sacrifice to the Lord during the day. I read in the Scriptures that Jesus taught us to fast and pray (Matt. 6:16; Mark 9:29). I had never fasted during my Christian life and could not go an entire day without food. Then I read in *The Diet Alternative* about the law of sowing and reaping taught in Galatians.[6]

> Do not be deceived, God is not mocked; for whatever a man sows, this he will also reap. For the one who sows to his own flesh will from the flesh reap corruption, but the one who sows to the Spirit will from the Spirit reap eternal life.
>
> —GALATIANS 6:7–8

I began to give up a certain food for a day to "sow" control into my eating habits. I expected to reap the benefits of overcoming the corruption of sowing to my flesh. Some time after the Lord showed me that I had a spirit of gluttony, Cal and I were again flying to a conference together. Before boarding the plane, I told the Lord I was going to give up those cookies as a sacrifice to Him in thanksgiving for being free from gluttony. When we were in the air and I saw the familiar snack cart coming up the aisle, my desire for those cookies almost overwhelmed me. However, true to my promise, when the steward asked if I wanted a cookie, I said politely, "No, thank you."

After the aisle was cleared a short time later, I got up to use the bathroom. Once inside that little room, I started crying. I could not believe it. I was sixty-four years old and crying because I did not get to eat those cookies. In my brokenness I said, "Lord, thank You for showing me how deep that awful spirit of gluttony had lodged in me. And thank You for Your wonderful deliverance."

I can say honestly that I have eaten those cookies on other flights since then, but on other occasions I have been free to pass them up as a sacrifice of thanksgiving to the Lord. To have the strength to say no is a wonderful sense of empowerment that the Holy Spirit has given me; I do not want to open any doors for the enemy to have access to that area of my life again.

My body is His temple.

I believe one of the most important things we need to remember is that, as Christians, our body is the temple of the Holy Spirit, and He needs us to be healthy. We will not be effective in His kingdom if we cannot move around or be available to do the work the Lord has called us to do. I have embraced this truth and made it my goal to glorify God in my body and my spirit:

> Or do you not know that your body is the temple of the Holy Spirit who is in you, whom you have from God, and you are not

your own? For you were bought at a price; therefore glorify God in your body and in your spirit, which are God's.

—1 CORINTHIANS 6:19–20, NKJV

When we allow ourselves to be enslaved by a person or behavior, we sin. When I first started sharing my testimony in conferences about being delivered from a spirit of gluttony, the Lord highlighted this scripture to me. It explained just what I was feeling when I was in bondage to that terrible thing. The apostle Paul was explaining the war that rages between our born-again spirit man and our unrenewed mind:

> I don't really understand myself, for I want to do what is right, but I don't do it. Instead, I do what I hate. But if I know that what I am doing is wrong, this shows that I agree that the law is good. So I am not the one doing wrong; it is sin living in me that does it. And I know that nothing good lives in me, that is, in my sinful nature. I want to do what is right, but I can't. I want to do what is good, but I don't. I don't want to do what is wrong, but I do it anyway. But if I do what I don't want to do, I am not really the one doing wrong; it is sin living in me that does it. I have discovered this principle of life—that when I want to do what is right, I inevitably do what is wrong. I love God's law with all my heart. But there is another power within me. Oh, what a miserable person I am! Who will free me from this life that is dominated by sin and death? Thank God! The answer is in Jesus Christ our Lord.
>
> —ROMANS 7:15–25, NLT

As we grow in our relationship with Christ, learning to yield to the Holy Spirit within, He helps us to receive the deliverance He purchased for us on the cross. The important thing to remember in receiving from God is to ask Him to forgive you and then forgive yourself. I understand that you have to make choices to pursue health and make changes to your lifestyle, but it is important to commit even those changes to God.

To keep from trying one more time in your own strength and failing, you must ask the Holy Spirit what He wants you to do. Then learn to wait and listen to His answer, and when it comes, do it. You can trust Him to lead you and then empower you to make the changes that will result in health for you. You have to settle it that you cannot continue to eat the way you have been eating. You may need to learn to eat the healthy foods that feed your body with good nutrition. You also need to be feeding your soul with the food of the Spirit from God's Word!

Testimony of Fruitfulness

The first time I shared my testimony of deliverance from a spirit of gluttony at a conference was in 2009 at the Spiritual Hunger Conference in Spokane, Washington. When I finished, I invited anyone who wanted to be set free from this kind of spiritual bondage to come forward, and I would help them pray a prayer to receive deliverance. A few months later we received an awesome testimony from a young woman who came forward that evening and prayed that prayer. I think her testimony will inspire you and build your faith:

> Last year I went to my first Spiritual Hunger Conference in Spokane. I didn't understand or even believe in divine healing at the time. During the course of the weekend, God met me in a powerful way, and I was healed of ailments in my feet, my knees, and my back. And I was baptized in the Holy Spirit and given my prayer language! It was *quite* a weekend for me!
>
> Also during the conference I received prayer regarding my addiction to food and need for weight loss. When I went home, the Lord began speaking to me about my eating. He wanted me to start *asking Him what I could eat*. I understood that I was to *just ask and listen—that was it*. I didn't think it would work at first, but eventually I gave in and tried it. Within a matter of days

my whole life in regard to food changed. Every time I asked what to eat and listened for His response, He *supplied me with the ability to carry it out.* All my cravings for bad food disappeared practically overnight! I knew I had truly been set free from my addiction to unhealthy foods.

Few people could understand my excitement at the beginning, but they sure can now: to date I have lost 118 pounds in ten months, simply by asking the Lord what I should eat and then doing it. I have never felt like I was on a diet or even felt deprived of anything I used to crave—I have been completely *set free from my food addiction!* The process has been so simple—whenever I'm faced with a food choice, I simply ask Him and He responds. If it's yes, I can eat *guilt free!* Even, occasionally, if I am asking about an unhealthy food and I sense His yes, I never get sick and I still lose weight!

And when He says no, I never feel deprived. It's easy to walk away—I don't even feel like I'm trying! God has done an amazing thing for me, and I can't seem to testify about it enough. In just one year my entire life has changed, and my relationship with God has deepened so much. And the best part—I could NEVER QUIT HIM! I could never walk away from His amazing love and delivering power! So this is it…it's really happening, and I have no doubts that I am done with my weight issue for the rest of my life! I'm just waiting for my body to catch up to that reality. Thank You, JESUS! Thank you to those who helped me along the way! PRAISE GOD—I'VE BEEN SET FREE!

—Renee Henderson
September 2, 2010

At the time of printing for this book, when I asked Renee if I could include her testimony in my chapter, she said yes. She added that to date she has lost 135 pounds and wants us to know that by the time this book comes out, she will have lost much more. We are praising God with Renee. He is good; He is faithful!

My Prayer for You

As I go about the country speaking about my life, so many people thank me for speaking candidly about a painful spiritual bondage that has not always been properly addressed in the church. I want you to know the freedom that I and others are experiencing as we face off with the spirit of gluttony, in the power of the Holy Spirit, and win! I am writing this chapter so that everyone who sees signs of the spirit of gluttony in their life can know how to be set free.

Writing this chapter has been very difficult for me. I have cried many times as I wrote about painful memories of my family, my husband, and especially my personal faulty walk with the Lord. I was a Christian for many years and still did not go to the Holy Spirit for help with this great need in my life, my weight issues.

However, more important than reliving that pain is the fact that I know I am free from the evil spirit that bound me for so many years, causing misery in my relationships and my walk with God. And I understand that my continued freedom is a result of keeping my relationship with food under the power of the blood of Jesus, who paid the price through His shed blood for my ultimate *victory*! My desire for you is that you can walk in this wonderful freedom from gluttony and see your entire life transformed.

To that end I have included a prayer to help you ask God to set you free. When you pray this prayer aloud, do so in faith, believing that as you pray, you are set free from the spirit of gluttony. I have shared promises from the Word of God that declare His will for you is your freedom. I have prayed this prayer. And I know that the *warfare* over my life regarding food is over forever. The deception is conquered each time I am tempted to hide food from my husband and I immediately go to him and tell him what I have done. Walking in the light with people who love me keeps the enemy from getting a foothold in that area of my life again.

I pray for everyone who is reading this chapter that the Lord will bring healing to you—*body, soul, and spirit!*

Prayer for Deliverance From Gluttony

- Heavenly Father, I repent for turning to anything other than You as my source.

- I repent for using food as my source of comfort and/or happiness.

- I repent for allowing my body to become addicted to food and then allowing that addiction to rule my choices.

- I repent for hiding this from others and burying it in the dark.

- I choose to live in light! I receive Your forgiveness through the blood of Jesus; I declare I am forgiven.

- I forgive my forefathers who lived in this same bondage; I forgive all those who have wounded me and brought pain into my life.

- I wash us all with the blood of Jesus, and we are all now purified of this unrighteousness, redeemed of the consequences, and restored to be the children of God we were created to be.

- I declare Your Word that says the accuser of the brethren has been cast down and that I have overcome him because of the blood of the Lamb and the word of my testimony (Rev. 12:10–11).

- I declare that the memory of these sins is erased.

- The curses are undone.

- I ask You, Father, to teach me new ways of thinking to replace these habits of eating.

- I cast every demon at the feet of Jesus; they have just lost their rights to torment me, and I tell them never to return.

- I give You the glory, Father, for setting me free. AMEN!

Declarations

- I declare that THE WAR IS WON!

- I declare that THE SPIRIT OF GLUTTONY NO LONGER LIVES IN ME!

- I declare that I NOW EAT TO LIVE—I DO NOT LIVE TO EAT!

Chapter 9

FULFILLING YOUR DESTINY

How you value your future "determines" your past.

Perhaps the subtitle to this chapter seems illogical, since we normally think that our *past* determines our *future*. Let me explain. Your past was determined by your understanding then of God's call to fulfill your destiny. The value you placed on your future in the past has determined your fulfillment of that God-given destiny to this point. As you increasingly value God's will for your life, your past becomes a testimony of what God has done as you manifest fulfillment of His destiny for your life. Fulfilling your projected destiny ultimately defines your past. Likewise, hurting people have a past that has been determined by their personal wrongdoing or their lack of understanding God's will for their lives.

Too many of God's people are not receiving breakthrough because they have not addressed the calling of God on their life. Many get born again and then begin a religious struggle to figure everything out. They attend church and sit in a pew as though that is what their destiny is to be. After a while they find themselves going to church simply because they have become personally needy.

This religious pattern becomes routine; you only have an encounter with *church* rather than with God. Church becomes "religious" when you know what is going to happen before you get there. You attend services, participate in worship, give an offering, hear announcements, listen to a teaching, but go home without being changed. In this scenario *church* is perceived as the "fixing place" rather than the equipping place of the saints for the work of the ministry (Eph. 4:12).

The problem is that you never get fixed because you have adopted a form of religion rather seeking the power of God.

Many then develop a mind-set that their destiny is to become born again and then take a beating from the devil the rest of their life. With that mentality, truth cannot set us free because we are not living in it. Instead we are trying to have the benefit of a kingdom we are not bringing to earth through faith. This religious scenario produces frustrated Christians. I have discovered that becoming born again and just settling for "being a Christian" will make a person miserable. We are not called to just be religious; we are called to establish the kingdom of God in the earth.

You cannot move in the fullness of destiny until you realize the value God places on the lost and the sick; they are worth laying down your life to be equipped to minister Christ's life to them. The truth is that when you are born again, you become a threat to the enemy. The Scriptures teach that the weapons of our warfare are mighty in God to tearing down the strongholds of the enemy (2 Cor. 10:4, NKJV). The enemy knows if he can keep your religion limited to sitting in a pew for one hour on Sunday, your destiny in God will be denied.

Do not get me wrong. I am not criticizing the church; I am speaking about the religious practices we call "church" that prevent people from having a true encounter with the living God that changes their lives. If the enemy can cause a Christian to be preoccupied with his destructive tactics, he can prevent them from being occupied with what God wants to do. A traumatized Christian will have a tendency to focus on the problems brought by the enemy. He defeats them by making them problem centered rather than God centered.

Our Calling

We cannot become victorious Christians until we understand our calling. It is our calling that releases our destiny in God. Our calling supplies the abundance of the kingdom of God to fulfill our destiny:

> Therefore, brethren, be all the more diligent to make certain about His *calling* and choosing you; for as long as you practice these things, you will *never stumble*; for in this way the entrance into the eternal kingdom of our Lord and Savior Jesus Christ will be abundantly supplied to you.
>
> —2 PETER 1:10–11, EMPHASIS ADDED

The word *calling* in the above verse is derived from a base verb that means "to be ordered or commanded."[1] It is a call for a believer to be positioned to receive their inheritance of the Word as they allow the Holy Spirit to order their steps. The psalmist declared, "The steps of a good man are ordered by the LORD: and he delighteth in his way" (Ps. 37:23, KJV). This Hebrew word *ordered* means "to direct aright, to establish, arrange, and securely determine."[2]

When a believer does not understand his calling, he becomes subject to strategy of the enemy rather than the other way around. It is in understanding our calling that the true knowledge of how to receive our inheritance through the will of God is released. Then we begin to move in the divine power of God to overcome the enemy. Without this understanding we lack the power to resist the evil one. The Word tells us if we are certain about our calling and practice what it brings, we will never stumble. The reason you will not stumble or fall is because your calling provides the entrance into the kingdom of God, where you will be abundantly supplied. You will not fall inside the kingdom; you only fall outside the kingdom.

God has not just called us to become Christians and then wait around for Jesus to return so that we receive our future inheritance after the Rapture, as I have discussed. We are called to be part of His army now. We are ordained to walk in the steps ordered and arranged for our lives by God Himself. We are called to be warriors who wear the armor of God and walk in truth to destroy the work of the enemy. Why do we destroy the work of the enemy? We do it to bring the kingdom of heaven on earth as it is in heaven. Peter explains what this looks like:

> Seeing that His divine power has granted to us everything pertaining to life and godliness, through the true knowledge of Him who called us by His own glory and excellence. For by these He has granted to us His precious and magnificent promises, so that by them you may become partakers of the divine nature, having escaped the corruption that is in the world by lust.
>
> —2 PETER 1:3–4

Peter declares that God's divine power has granted to us everything we need that pertains to our life and godliness. That divine power is the Spirit of God in us. He gives us *everything* we need, not just some things. We cannot complain that our life is not victorious because He only gives us some things. We are given everything we need through the true knowledge of Him who calls us.

Lots of people, even those who are living in bondage, have knowledge. But according to this scripture, *true* knowledge comes from God. We can become theologians to try to gain lots of knowledge about the Bible. This information will not keep us from stumbling. Only by the true knowledge of Christ and Him crucified can we receive divine power to defeat the enemy and walk in victory.

These promises are not given so that we can have a lot of knowledge. They are given so that we can be "partakers of the divine nature" of God. His divine nature is not sin and sickness; it is divine health. This is what we are to partake of. The Greek word for *partakers* in 2 Peter 1:4 means "a sharer; a partner."[3] We are to partner with the

Holy Spirit, who provides the divine power of God to live in wholeness. That is how we will escape the corruption that is in the world. It cannot overtake us when we partner with God; we will escape it.

The key to our escaping corruption in the world is to understand that we are called by God and have been given His divine power for everything we need to live life in His kingdom. Peter tells believers to apply all diligence to our faith to walk in these promises:

> Now for this very reason also, applying all diligence, in your faith supply moral excellence, and in your moral excellence, knowledge, and in your knowledge, self-control, and in your self-control, perseverance, and in your perseverance, godliness, and in your godliness, brotherly kindness, and in your brotherly kindness, love.
>
> —2 Peter 1:5–7

The Holy Spirit empowers us to receive the fruit of His Spirit for our lives. When we embrace Him, His fruit is available to us. As we walk in the Spirit, we receive His divine nature that provides the Christlike character of diligence, faith, moral excellence, knowledge, self-control, perseverance, godliness, brotherly kindness, and love. These are the qualities each believer receives by partnering with the Spirit of God. When we partner with Him and live by these qualities, we will never stumble. It is these attributes that are abundantly supplied to us by Jesus Christ; we cannot cultivate them in our own strength. This true godliness is something we should strive to see fulfilled in our lives.

Rapture Mentality Versus Harvest Theology

Earlier I mentioned the faulty "Rapture mentality" that plagues many Christians. There is a lot of talk about the Rapture among Christians. Some people are predicting when it will happen. I have noticed when things tend to look worse in the world, people talk more about the

Rapture. There's less talk about it when things look good, more talk when things look bad. It seems that we do not mind hanging around in this world during the good times; we just do not want to be here in the bad times.

The Scriptures teach clearly that Jesus is returning for His bride. But the question is, what is His bride supposed to be doing when He does return—sitting around waiting? Jesus did not command us to "Go into all the world and wait." He said:

> And as you go, preach, saying, "The kingdom of heaven is at hand. Heal the sick, raise the dead, cleanse the lepers, cast out demons. Freely you received, freely give."
> —MATTHEW 10:7–8

We are not to be a hearer of the Word only, waiting for something to happen. We are to be a doer of the Word, making something happen by the power of the Holy Spirit. We cannot live in the fullness of our earthly destiny if we put our focus on a *Rapture* instead of a harvest. A Rapture mentality will cause us to look only for a future kingdom and not to the kingdom that Jesus wants us to bring on the earth.

We cannot deny that Jesus said to go into all the world and preach the gospel of the kingdom to the lost. Our destiny is to witness to the lost generation regarding the kingdom of God. If we do not focus on this present harvest, we will focus on the future Rapture. Remember, Jesus said that the kingdom of God is within us (Luke 17:21, NKJV). And Paul describes the kingdom of God as "righteousness and peace and joy in the Holy Spirit" (Rom. 14:17).

You will not recognize the kingdom of God within you if you are looking somewhere else for it. Our destiny is releasing the power of the kingdom within us to fulfill the Great Commission and prepare for the kingdom in our future.

A harvest theology will bring the kingdom of heaven upon the earth. Jesus was bringing the kingdom of God to earth so that the harvest would be reaped. He came as our Redeemer to set us free from sin and death. We have been granted everything we need pertaining to life and godliness, but are we receiving that? The provision of God, His Word, His Spirit, His anointing, His armor, and His power (authority) are provided to the believer for the purpose of redeeming His children. Then we are called to reap a harvest of souls for His kingdom. God so loved the world that He gave His Son for it (John 3:16).

Our Purpose

Too many believers are not fulfilling their destiny because they do not understand their purpose. Kingdom provision comes by way of understanding our purpose. Without purpose we are like fish out of water. We do not have what we need to move properly. The fish cannot swim on the bank. His purpose is fulfilled in a water environment. As Christians, we have no purpose if we live outside the environment of God's kingdom. When I was first born again, I thought I was saved "to have a life"—*my* life under my direction. Unfortunately, with that approach to my Christian life, I was like the proverbial fish out of water. Nothing worked in my Christian environment when I was directing my life. Over the years some of the most miserable people I have met have been people who thought they had a life as well, a life to direct as they chose.

I had all these things in my life that I was hanging on to. I began to notice that those were the things the devil could attack. A good example was my finances. Because I "had a life," my money was mine. I did not live to give. Yet I was never able to prosper with the money I hung on to. The devil was always able to rob and steal what I had. When I began to understand it was not about my life, it was about the life of Christ in me, I learned that I could put my finances into the kingdom purposes where the enemy could no longer have access to them (Mal. 3:8–12).

Too many Christians are having problems because their lives aren't directed by God into His glorious liberty. When I realized that *my* purpose was that I was called to *God's* purpose, my provision was no longer based on what I had but on what God has to give to me. When God is our source, then all things work for our redemption and freedom in Christ.

> And we know that God causes *all things* to work together for good to those who love God, to those who are called according to *His purpose.*
> —ROMANS 8:28, EMPHASIS ADDED

When we walk in God's purpose for our life, He causes all things to work for our good. When we love God and are called to His purpose, His kingdom provision becomes available. God's ultimate purpose in sending Christ to the earth is expressed powerfully in 1 John 3:8: "The Son of God appeared for this purpose, to destroy the works of the devil."

We, as the body of Christ, are called to fulfill His purpose to destroy the works of the devil. We are called to bring the kingdom of heaven to earth—to heal the sick, raise the dead, cleanse the lepers, and cast out demons. This is our purpose. It is this purpose that provides the authority of God for every believer to walk victoriously.

Without understanding kingdom purpose, we become subject to the purpose of the world. The enemy's purpose is "to steal and kill and destroy" in the world (John 10:10). Our purpose will either be God's purpose or the purpose of the enemy. Without God's purpose, we will be driven by the purpose of the enemy. The purpose of the enemy is all about trouble. His goal is fulfilled when trouble affects our lives negatively. The enemy wants to steal our purpose in God by fulfilling his purpose in us. He brings trouble in our bodies, in our marriages, in our finances, in our churches, and in our cities. When these things cause us to be troubled and fearful, we are moved away from being peaceful and faithful. We forfeit the promises of God for our lives.

> Peace I leave with you; My peace I give to you; not as the world gives do I give to you. Do not let your heart be troubled, nor let it be fearful.
>
> —JOHN 14:27

How can we destroy the work of the enemy when the work of the enemy is destroying us? This is a huge issue in the church today. We have been kept busy fighting our own problems and not moving in our destiny. The enemy uses trouble to produce fear. When fear motivates us, we transfer our authority over to the enemy.

When a believer lives in fear, their words become creative in the enemy's camp. Their confession will line up with his will, not God's. For example, people say things like: "I am sick." "I am broke." "My marriage is bad." "I do not like that person." "My life is a mess; I am in turmoil." In each of these statements the person takes possession of something that is not the will of God. It is all right to recognize where the problem is, but why take possession of it as though it *belongs* to us? What the enemy does should only be a target for what God does through the believer. Our destiny is to find the target, bring the kingdom, and destroy the enemy's work.

Authority to Rule

Earlier I discussed God's original purpose for mankind, that we are created in God's image and likeness to rule over all the earth (Gen. 1:26). This was man's mandate in the beginning; it was a dominion mandate. When the Creator gives dominion, it comes with authority to rule. If we do not have authority, we will not move in dominion power. Our destiny must come with rulership. Authority provides the power to rule. Jesus has restored our rulership in the earth:

> And He put all things in subjection under His feet, and gave Him as head over all things to the church, which is His body, the fullness of Him who fills all in all.
>
> —EPHESIANS 1:22–23

Jesus is the head over all things to the church, which is His body. As members of His body, our dominion mandate comes from the head, Jesus. This is why Jesus could declare: "Behold, I have given you authority…" (Luke 10:19). We are now under the head, who is Jesus. His authority flows down through His body so we can establish His kingdom on earth as it is in heaven. Our destiny is to be the rule and reign of God on the earth. The same power of the Holy Spirit that provides authority to us also provides power in us. It is this supernatural power that can quicken our mortal bodies to walk in health.

20/20 Vision

Vision is an important part of walking into our destiny. We are not talking about natural vision; we are talking about kingdom vision. We cannot go anywhere without vision. God gives us vision so that we can see what is in our future. Without kingdom vision, we are restrained. We cannot see anything happening because we only see what exists now. When things now do not provide answers, we begin to doubt and perish in failure:

> Where there is no vision, the people perish.
>
> —PROVERBS 29:18, KJV

Without kingdom vision, we cannot see what God is doing; we only see what the enemy is doing. When we walk by sight in the natural, we deny kingdom vision; in the kingdom of God, vision establishes sight. The Greek word for *vision* in Proverbs 29:18 can be translated "revelation; divine communication."[4] When we partner with the Holy Spirit, He provides the revelation that shows us our future destiny. Vision allows you to see where you are going. Faith says, "I trust the Holy Spirit to lead me." The Holy Spirit gives us vision to establish God's kingdom on earth. Vision that is Spirit-driven sees what is not so that it can be. Divine vision sees a kingdom reality waiting to happen. Our vision will use the resources of heaven to carry the will of God from heaven to earth. Vision sees what is fulfilled in heaven waiting for fulfillment on earth. Kingdom vision is God's provision for all believers. Vision sets the mind on the things above, not on the things of earth.

Things seen in the natural realm will not produce vision because they already exist. It does not take faith to believe what is seen. Kingdom vision brings ideas. Ideas are containers for the will of God to fill. A good idea is a God idea. Kingdom vision will not make sense to a natural mind. Vision becomes a reality in your life when you walk by faith. When you have kingdom vision, the existence of what you do not see is greater than the existence of what you do see in the natural. Natural sight looks for it and says it is not here; a vision of faith confesses the truth that is not seen so that it can appear.

When vision is established in your heart by the Spirit of God, it sees the will of God coming. Kingdom vision sees with the mind of Christ. Jesus said, "He who has seen Me has seen the Father" (John 14:9). All vision is God's reality yet unseen by natural sight. Vision must come supernaturally by the Spirit of God to the spirit of man. Kingdom vision cannot become reality in the natural realm unless the mind is set to it. Instead of being conformed to the world, the mind must be transformed by kingdom vision. The vision of what God allows you to see is greater reality than that which you are trying to transform. If you need vision, you can ask the Holy Spirit for it; He is a visionary.

A New Sound

There is sound everywhere on the earth: city sounds, country sounds, animal sounds, water sounds, wind sounds, people sounds, and so forth. Movement produces sound, and sound can produce movement. In Genesis God used sound when He spoke to bring all of creation into existence. Sound can be creative or it can be destructive. God uses sound to establish His kingdom through the body of Christ. The enemy uses sound to try and tear it down. The sound of heaven is creative; the sound of hell is destructive.

When a person speaks words that tear down, they are establishing (creating) the will of the enemy. In healing rooms we see thousands of people who are suffering from trauma because of words spoken to them that were hurtful. We have seen people who have carried hurts their entire lives because of hearing a "sound" that was meant to create pain.

Our destiny is to become the sound of truth upon the earth. The sound we make must create by the power and will of God. If you think about it, the will of God must be heard on the earth so that it can be fulfilled. The Word produces faith. Faith is the substance of things hoped for (Heb. 11:1, NKJV). Faith requires us to confess or speak those things that are not as though they were. If we need someone to be healed, it is not enough to think they can be healed; we must speak out of our faith the sound, "Be healed." The Word of God must be heard by man to enter his heart; then it must be spoken to enter into the world. When the world hears the sound of God's will, His healing and restoration take place. The will of God—when received by hearing—edifies, builds up, and restores. When spoken, it brings the grace of God to lives.

> Let no unwholesome word proceed from your mouth, but only such a word as is good for edification according to the need of the moment, that it may give grace to those who hear.
>
> —EPHESIANS 4:29

What we say, the sound we release, must be produced by the will of God, motivated to give life by the Spirit of God. According to the Scriptures, as I have mentioned, our words have the power of life or death (Prov. 18:21).

If we are to walk in the fullness of divine authority, we must know how to obtain health in our spirit, our mind, and our body. A Spirit-led man must bring a new sound upon the earth. It must be the sound that edifies and restores those who need to hear what God is saying: "The tongue of the wise brings healing" (Prov. 12:18). We must have the wisdom to speak good words that heal. And our life-style must reflect what we speak. The power of God must change us before it can change them.

The "Last Chapter"

As I began to write the last chapter of this book, the Holy Spirit said to me, "My church is in the last chapter." We are quickly entering into a season where business as usual in the church will no longer do, a season where we either overcome by our God or we will be overcome by our enemy. There will be no middle ground. We are quickly entering into the season where everything that can be shaken will be shaken.

> And His voice shook the earth then, but now He has promised, saying, "Yet once more I will shake not only the earth, but also the heaven." This expression, "Yet once more," denotes the removing of those things which can be shaken, as of created things, so that those things which cannot be shaken may remain.
> —HEBREWS 12:26–27

This passage is a warning to the end-time church that there will not be any escape for those who turn away from God and His truth: "For if those did not escape when they refused him who warned them on earth, much less shall we escape who turn away from Him who warns from heaven" (v. 25). We cannot ride out the storm when our boat is sinking. Our boat is our will, our life under our direction. Walking in His will, we will not even need a boat because we can walk on water if the need arises; all things are possible to those who believe God.

This will be a time when God's people have to decide whether to hear the sounds of heaven or the sounds of earth. To survive the shaking, we must hear what the Spirit is saying and heed His voice: "See to it that you do not refuse Him who is speaking" (v. 25). We must not allow religious mind-sets to prevent us from hearing what God is speaking. The season of shaking will be the preparation for the dread champions Jeremiah spoke of:

> But the LORD is with me like a *dread* champion; therefore my persecutors will stumble and not prevail. They will be utterly ashamed, because they have failed, with an everlasting disgrace that will not be forgotten.
>
> —JEREMIAH 20:11, EMPHASIS ADDED

The God who was with Jeremiah is the same God who is with us. The reason He is with us is because He is in us. He is the source of our victory, making our enemy dread us. The Hebrew word translated "dread" means "mighty, terrible one, powerful, strong and violent."[5] As end-time warriors, we will put fear in the enemy's camp because we will carry the awesome presence of God. We will release the kingdom of heaven everywhere we go. Our enemy will not prevail because there is no prevailing against a God-occupied man.

The shakings of God in the world will result in these end-time warriors who walk in the light of God amid great darkness in the earth. The prophet Isaiah declared this end-time reality:

> Arise, shine; for your light has come, and the glory of the LORD has risen upon you. For behold, darkness will cover the earth

and deep darkness the peoples; but the LORD will rise upon you
and His glory will appear upon you.

—ISAIAH 60:1–2

Today Christians everywhere whom we encounter have questions
about what is happening in the world today. In their questions we can
hear the fear they are feeling. They live in a comfort zone and do not
want the boat to rock. Yet God's Word promises that everything that
can be shaken will be shaken. Our comfort zone is going to be shaken.
Why? Because God is saying that He only wants those things that are
of Him to remain in our lives. Everything else must go. We are a new
creation; old things are to pass away so that the new things God has
ordained can come to pass.

Is there a shaking going on in the earth today? Is our comfort zone
starting to shrink? As I am writing this book, the world economies
are moving from recession to inflation. People in nations are rebel-
ling against their leadership because of unemployment and poverty.
The World Bank is saying we are in danger of a worldwide food crisis.
Pandemics of disease, obesity, and infectious viruses are happening
at an increasing rate. Catastrophic storms are creating flooding, fires,
and record snows in places where we have not ever seen them in that
degree. In the United States, state, county, and city governments are
experiencing budget crises that are jeopardizing their ability to provide needed social services. The structure of what defines a "godly
family" is being attacked.

How long can we turn a deaf ear to Him who is speaking to His
bride? We must no longer ignore the warning signs before us. Our
destiny lies before us. We must step into it. The kingdom of God is
waiting for those who will lay down their life to become a "dread
champion."

> Therefore, since we receive a kingdom which cannot be shaken, let us show gratitude, by which we may offer to God an acceptable service with reverence and awe; for our God is a consuming fire.
> —HEBREWS 12:28–29

When we allow God to remove the things in our life that can be shaken, we receive a kingdom that cannot be shaken. With receiving an unshakable kingdom, we have His ability to offer an acceptable service. The Greek word for *acceptable* means "in a manner well pleasing."[6] We are only well pleasing to God when our will becomes His will. This is the fullness of destiny, where we no longer refuse to hear what He is speaking.

Our Brightest Hour

I believe we are entering into the brightest hour the church has ever seen. God's people need end-time revelation to see God's victory; we are not supposed to be the losers here. I quoted this previously, but I want to do so again here, adding verse 3.

> Arise, shine; for your light has come, and the glory of the LORD has risen upon you. For behold, darkness will cover the earth and deep darkness the peoples; but the LORD will rise upon you and His glory will appear upon you. Nations will come to your light, and kings to the *brightness* of your rising.
> —ISAIAH 60:1–3, EMPHASIS ADDED

Isaiah speaks powerfully here to the modern-day church as well as to the people of his day. He speaks of the will of God for His people then and to believers now. He prophesies that when darkness covers the earth, the glory of God will appear upon His people. The Hebrew word *kabowd* is translated as "glory," which means "weight" or "splendor."[7] It is the manifestation of His splendor upon His bride to bring His kingdom to the earth. The light of God will illuminate His people with His glory so that they become the light of the world.

These end-time warriors will be carriers of truth absolute. They will carry the only answer left that can give deliverance to people. These kingdom warriors will speak with such authority that their words will go out with fulfillment in them and not return void. As they speak the will of God, angels will be sent out to complete what they say:

> Bless the LORD, you His angels, mighty in strength, who perform His word.
>
> —PSALM 103:20

The enemy will not be able to prevail against these dread champions because they will not move by their authority but by God in them, who is all authority. The glory of God, the light who is God, will be so bright upon them that nations will seek their counsel. These warriors will carry God's government to nations. God's kingdom is His government. Again it was Isaiah who prophesied of this divine government:

> For a child will be born to us, a son will be given to us; and the government will rest on His shoulders; and His name will be called Wonderful Counselor, Mighty God, Eternal Father, Prince of Peace. There will be no end to the increase of His government or of peace...
>
> —ISAIAH 9:6–7

Jesus is seated at the right hand of God, and we are His body in the earth. He has given us authority to establish His kingdom, His government in the earth. The key to Isaiah's prophecy in chapter 60 is in the first word: *Arise*. The Hebrew word for *arise* means "to stir up, strengthen, abide in, accomplish and to decree."[8] The call to arise is not for everyone; it is for Christ's body. Someone has said that God cannot steer a parked car. As believers, we must begin to move, to stir ourselves to be a part of what He is doing in the earth.

If you want a move of God, remember, His Spirit dwells within you. Start moving. In faith begin to arise, because your light *has* come. It didn't say your light might come; it is waiting for a moving vehicle. We are not to be hearers of the Word only, but also doers (James 1:22). We are supposed to preach the good news to every creature. This is not the time to sit around and be fearful. The enemy wants the church to be fearful. He knows that if we are fearful, we will not be faithful to do God's will. The enemy does not want us to move into our destiny. He knows that fear will steal our peace. The Scriptures teach clearly that we are not to give place to fear:

> Do not be afraid of sudden fear nor of the onslaught of the wicked when it comes; for the LORD will be your confidence and will keep your foot from being caught.
>
> —PROVERBS 3:25–26

God has called us to peace, not to fear (1 Cor. 7:15). We are not to let the condition of the world affect our position of victory in God. The promise of God is that He will be our confidence and will keep our feet from being tripped up. He will be our provision because He is our divine provider. If we are not afraid, the peace of God will guard our hearts from what the enemy does to frighten us.

> And the peace of God, which surpasses all comprehension, will guard your hearts and your minds in Christ Jesus.
>
> —PHILIPPIANS 4:7

We are promised the *peace of God* to guard our hearts and our minds. It is not our peace; it is God's supernatural peace, which will surpass *all* comprehension. God can give us a perfect peace in any storm.

A Kingdom Company

God is looking for a kingdom company, that is, a company of kingdom-minded people who have decided to be overcomers. They will overcome their enemy by being overcome by their God. They will demonstrate a dominion demeanor; they will have a godly confidence. They will no longer teach by word only but by a demonstration of power. They will understand their true identity in Christ Jesus, which will allow them to walk in divine destiny: "For in Him all the fullness of the Deity dwells in bodily form, and in Him you have been made complete..." (Col. 2:9–10).

This end-time kingdom company will walk complete in Christ as He is complete. We lack nothing at all as we abide in Him. Our true identity is that we are called to success, to walk in overcoming victory, fulfilling the Word that says, "As He is, so also are we in this world" (1 John 4:17). A kingdom company can identify with Christ because they are the body of Christ. This company will move in an acceptable time.

> Thus says the LORD: "In an acceptable time I have heard You, and in the day of salvation I have helped You; I will preserve You and give You as a covenant to the people, to *restore the earth*, to cause them to inherit the desolate heritages."
> —ISAIAH 49:8, NKJV, EMPHASIS ADDED

The reason we are to bring the kingdom of God to earth, as it is in heaven, is to restore the earth. The word *desolate* refers to all that has been devastated, deserted, and laid waste.[9] The word *heritages* refers to something inherited or occupied.[10] Now is the time to believe God's Word that tells you who you are in Christ. You must grasp the promises of God concerning your destiny through Christ. The Word declares that you are more than a conqueror; you must begin conquering. Your life is either going to be a series of testimonies gained from battles won or a list of regrets from your past failures. Your divine destiny is to bring God's kingdom economy to the earth as it is in heaven.

As part of the body of Christ, we are to be a covenant people who restore the desolate heritages of our lives and the lives of others. We are in the world but not of the world (John 17:14–16). We occupy to bring the kingdom or government of God to the earth as we fulfill His will. Our life should be a testimony of how to live an overcoming life:

> For whatever is born of God overcomes the world; and this is the *victory* that has overcome the world—our faith.
>
> —1 JOHN 5:4, EMPHASIS ADDED

We must become an example to the people of the world of how to get the victory. In the world, victory is declared when you win. In the kingdom, victory is *who you are*. We are not to battle for victory; we are to battle from victory. Do you qualify for the victory? Do you know the truth that sets you free? The same unlimited power of God that raised Jesus from the dead is at work in you to overcome every evil set against you. All you have to do is arise and shine, because the glory of the Lord is rising upon you.

You can live in the fullness of your destiny because Jesus is not only the author of your faith, but He is also the finisher or perfecter of your faith (Heb. 12:2). He authored a kingdom in heaven, and He wants to finish His kingdom on earth—in you and through you. Amen!

Notes

Chapter 1
The Condition of the Body

1. Centers for Disease Control and Prevention, "FastStats: Obesity and Overweight," June 18, 2010, http://www.cdc.gov/nchs/fastats/overwt.htm (accessed September 14, 2011).

2. B. Sherry, H. M. Blanck, D. A. Galuska, et al., "Vital Signs: State-Specific Obesity Prevalence Among Adults—United States, 2009," *Morbidity and Mortality Weekly Report (MMWR)* 59 (August 3, 2010): 1–5, http://www.cdc.gov/mmwr/preview/mmwrhtml/mm59e0803a1.htm (accessed September 14, 2011).

3. Ibid.

4. E. A. Finkelstein, J. G. Trogdon, J. W. Cohen, and W. Dietz, "Annual Medical Spending Attributable to Obesity: Payer- and Service-Specific Estimates," *Health Affairs* 28, no. 5 (2009): w822–w831, referenced in Centers for Disease and Prevention, "Overweight and Obesity: Economic Consequences," March 28, 2011, http://www.cdc.gov/obesity/causes/economics.html (accessed September 14, 2011).

5. As referenced in John Casey, "The Hidden Ingredient That Can Sabotage Your Diet," MedicineNet.com, January 3, 2005, http://www.medicinenet.com/script/main/art.asp?articlekey=56589 (accessed September 14, 2011).

6. Ibid.

7. AstroNutrition, "Dangers of Refined Sugar," *AstroNutrition's Blogs*, August 7, 2007, http://astronutrition.com/blog/dangers_of_refined_sugar (accessed September 14, 2011).

8. Biblesoft's *New Exhaustive Strong's Numbers and Concordance With Expanded Greek-Hebrew Dictionary*, PC Study Bible 3, copyright © 1994 Biblesoft and International Bible Translators, Inc., s.v. "*sozo*," NT:4982.

9. *Merriam-Webster's Collegiate Dictionary*, 9th ed. (Springfield, MA: Merriam-Webster, Inc., n.d.), s.v. "heal."

10. Ibid., s.v. "health."

11. Ibid., s.v. "healing."

12. Biblesoft's *New Exhaustive Strong's Numbers and Concordance With Expanded Greek-Hebrew Dictionary*, PC Study Bible 3, s.v. "*marpe*," OT:4832.

13. Ibid., s.v. "*therapeia*," NT:2322.

14. *Merriam-Webster's Collegiate Dictionary*, s.v. "therapy."

15. Biblesoft's *New Exhaustive Strong's Numbers and Concordance With Expanded Greek-Hebrew Dictionary*, PC Study Bible 3, s.v. "*choliy*," OT:2483.

16. Ibid., s.v. "*makob*," OT:4341.

17. Ibid., s.v. "*chay*," OT:2416.

Chapter 2
My Journey

1. Biblesoft's *New Exhaustive Strong's Numbers and Concordance With Expanded Greek-Hebrew Dictionary*, PC Study Bible 3, s.v. "*thanatos*," NT:2288.

2. Healthy Exercise World, "Antiaging Exercise," http://www .healthyexerciseworld.com/antiaging-exercise.html (accessed September 15, 2011).

3. Biblesoft's *New Exhaustive Strong's Numbers and Concordance With Expanded Greek-Hebrew Dictionary*, PC Study Bible 3, s.v. "*endunamoo*," NT:1743.

4. Ibid., s.v. "*anthistemi*," NT:436.

5. Synergy Worldwide, "Ron Williams," http://synergyworldwide.com/ Content.aspx?PageID=219 (accessed September 15, 2011).

6. Ron Williams, *Faith and Fat Loss* (Salt Lake City, UT: RTW Publishing International, 2009).

7. Biblesoft's *New Exhaustive Strong's Numbers and Concordance With Expanded Greek-Hebrew Dictionary*, PC Study Bible 3, s.v. "*hupomone*," NT:5281.

Chapter 3
God's Will for His Body

1. Eric Mankin, "Could People Live to 120?", *Albion Monitor*, May 27, 1996, http://www.albionmonitor.com/5-27-96/agingmax.html (accessed September 15, 2011).

2. Biblesoft's *New Exhaustive Strong's Numbers and Concordance With Expanded Greek-Hebrew Dictionary*, PC Study Bible 3, s.v. "*basar*," OT:1320.

3. Ibid., s.v. "*sarx*," NT:4561.

4. Ibid., s.v. "*metanoeo*," NT:3340.

5. F. F. Bruce, *The Acts of the Apostles: The Greek Text With Introduction and Commentary*, third ed. (Grand Rapids, MI: Wm. B. Eerdmans Publishing Company, 1990), 129.

6. Biblesoft's *New Exhaustive Strong's Numbers and Concordance With Expanded Greek-Hebrew Dictionary*, PC Study Bible 3, s.v. "*dikaiosune*," NT:1343.

7. Ibid., s.v. "*pleroo*," NT:4137.

8. Ibid., s.v. "*ktisis*," NT:2937.

9. Ibid., s.v. "*ktaomai*," NT:2932.

10. Ibid., s.v. "*phtheiro*," NT:5351.

11. Ibid., s.v. "*kaphar*," OT:3722.

12. Ibid., s.v. "*rapha*," OT:7465.

13. Ibid., s.v. "*zoopoieo*," NT:2227.

14. Ibid., s.v. "*sozo*," NT:4982.

15. Ibid., s.v. "*haplous*," NT:573.

16. Ibid., s.v. "*photeinos*," NT:5460.

17. Ibid., s.v. "*phos*," NT:5457.

Chapter 4
Truth That Overcomes Facts

1. Biblesoft's *New Exhaustive Strong's Numbers and Concordance With Expanded Greek-Hebrew Dictionary*, PC Study Bible 3, s.v. "*sunepimartureo*," NT:4901.

2. Ibid., s.v. "*elpizo*," NT:1679.

3. Ibid., s.v. "*yachal*," OT:3176.

4. Ibid., s.v. "*nike*," NT:3529.

5. Ibid., s.v. "*apodeixis*," NT:585.

Chapter 5
Partnering With the Holy Spirit

1. Biblesoft's *New Exhaustive Strong's Numbers and Concordance With Expanded Greek-Hebrew Dictionary*, PC Study Bible 3, s.v. "*hagios*," NT:40.

2. Ibid., s.v. "*hupomone*," NT:5281.

3. Ibid., s.v. "*chrisma*," NT:5545.

4. Ibid., s.v. "*tom*," OT:8537.

5. Ibid., s.v. "*proton*," NT:4412.

6. Ibid., s.v. "*zeteo*," NT:2212.

7. *Merriam-Webster's Collegiate Dictionary*, s.v. "dis-."

Chapter 6
Kingdom Authority

1. Biblesoft's *New Exhaustive Strong's Numbers and Concordance With Expanded Greek-Hebrew Dictionary*, PC Study Bible 3, s.v. "*exousia*," NT:1849.

2. Ibid., s.v. "*dunamis*," NT:1411.

3. Ibid., s.v. "*metanoeo*," NT:3340.

4. Ibid., s.v. "*katallasso*," NT:2644.

5. Ibid., s.v. "*diakrino*," NT:1252.

6. Ibid., s.v. "*shalowm*," OT:7965.

7. *Merriam-Webster's Collegiate Dictionary*, s.v. "breakthrough."

Chapter 7
Your Personal Health Care System

1. Sandra Hendrickson, "6 Dangers of Processed Foods for Your Kids," *Zis Boom Bah* (blog), May 11, 2011, http://blog.zisboombah.com/2011/05/11/why-whole-is-better-than-processed-food/ (accessed September 21, 2011).

2. Global Healing Center, "Daily Toxin Intake," http://www.globalhealingcenter.com/daily-toxin-intake.html (accessed September 21, 2011).

3. Brett Blumenthal, "8 Shocking Facts About Sugar," *Sheer Balance* (blog), http://www.sheerbalance.com/nutrition/8-shocking-facts-about-sugar/ (accessed September 21, 2011).

4. Ibid.

5. Centers for Disease Control and Prevention, "Number of People With Diabetes Increases to 24 Million," press release, June 24, 2008, http://www.cdc.gov/media/pressrel/2008/r080624.htm (accessed September 21, 2011).

6. Nanci Hellmich, "Obesity Is a Key Link to Soaring Health Tab," *USA Today*, http://www.usatoday.com/printedition/news/20090728/1aobesity28_st.art.htm (accessed September 21, 2011).

7. Robert Longley, "Aging Baby Boomers Flocking to Doctors," US Government Info, About.com, http://usgovinfo.about.com/cs/healthmedical/a/aasickboomers.htm (accessed September 21, 2011).

8. Centers for Disease Control and Prevention, "U.S. Obesity Trends," http://www.cdc.gov/obesity/data/trends.html (accessed September 21, 2011).

9. *Merriam-Webster's Collegiate Dictionary*, s.v. "poverty."

10. Elizabeth Scott, "Stress: How It Affects Your Body, and How You Can Stay Healthier," Stress Management, About.com, May 14, 2011, http://stress.about.com/od/stresshealth/a/stresshealth.htm (accessed September 22, 2011).

11. Biblesoft's *New Exhaustive Strong's Numbers and Concordance With Expanded Greek-Hebrew Dictionary*, PC Study Bible 3, s.v. "*eirene*," NT:1515.

12. Wayne L. Westcott, "Strength Training Changes Lives of 90-Year-Old Nursing Home Patients," Wellness.MA, http://www.wellness.ma/senior-fitness/senior-strength-training-90-year-olds.htm (accessed September 22, 2011).

13. Ibid.

14. Ibid.

15. Biblesoft's *New Exhaustive Strong's Numbers and Concordance With Expanded Greek-Hebrew Dictionary*, PC Study Bible 3, s.v. "*avon*," OT:5771.

16. Ibid., s.v. "*phos*," NT:5457.

Chapter 8
Overcoming the Spirit of Gluttony

1. *Merriam-Webster's Collegiate Dictionary*, s.v. "addiction."

2. Diane Hampton, *The Diet Alternative* (New Kensington, PA: Whitaker House, 1984), 17–23.

3. *Merriam-Webster's Collegiate Dictionary*, s.v. "gluttony."

4. Ibid., s.v. "glutton."

5. Biblesoft's *New Exhaustive Strong's Numbers and Concordance With Expanded Greek-Hebrew Dictionary*, PC Study Bible 3, s.v. "*yarash*," OT:3423.

6. Hampton, *The Diet Alternative*, 31.

Chapter 9
Fulfilling Your Destiny

1. Biblesoft's *New Exhaustive Strong's Numbers and Concordance With Expanded Greek-Hebrew Dictionary*, PC Study Bible 3, s.v. "*kelelu*," NT:2753.

2. Ibid., s.v. "*kuwn*," OT:3559.

3. Ibid., s.v. "*koinonos*," NT:2844.

4. Ibid., s.v. "*chazown*," OT:2377.

5. Ibid., s.v. "*ariyts*," OT:6184.

6. Ibid., s.v. "*euarestos*," NT:2102.

7. Ibid., s.v. "*kabowd*," OT:3519.

8. Ibid., s.v. "*quwm*," OT:6965.

9. Ibid., s.v. "*shamem*," OT:8074.

10. Ibid., s.v. "*nachalah*," OT:5159.

OTHER RESOURCES
BY CAL PIERCE

Books
Preparing the Way—the Healing Rooms Story
Healing in the Kingdom

Booklets
Healing in the Atonement
Roadblocks to Healing
Healing the Process to Establish Divine Health
Healing the Land
The Anointing that Empowers the Word
God's Power of Creation for the Miraculous
Apostolic Government
The Third Day Church
Breaking the Deaf and Dumb Spirit
Power Quotes

CDs
Restoring Your Health
Stepping Into Your Destiny (by Michelle Pierce)
Unveiled No Longer Afraid (by Michelle Pierce)

*Visit our website at www.healingrooms.com to order
the above products or for more information.*